THAI FOOD SENSATION

think Thai think fresh

SHAYNE AUSTIN

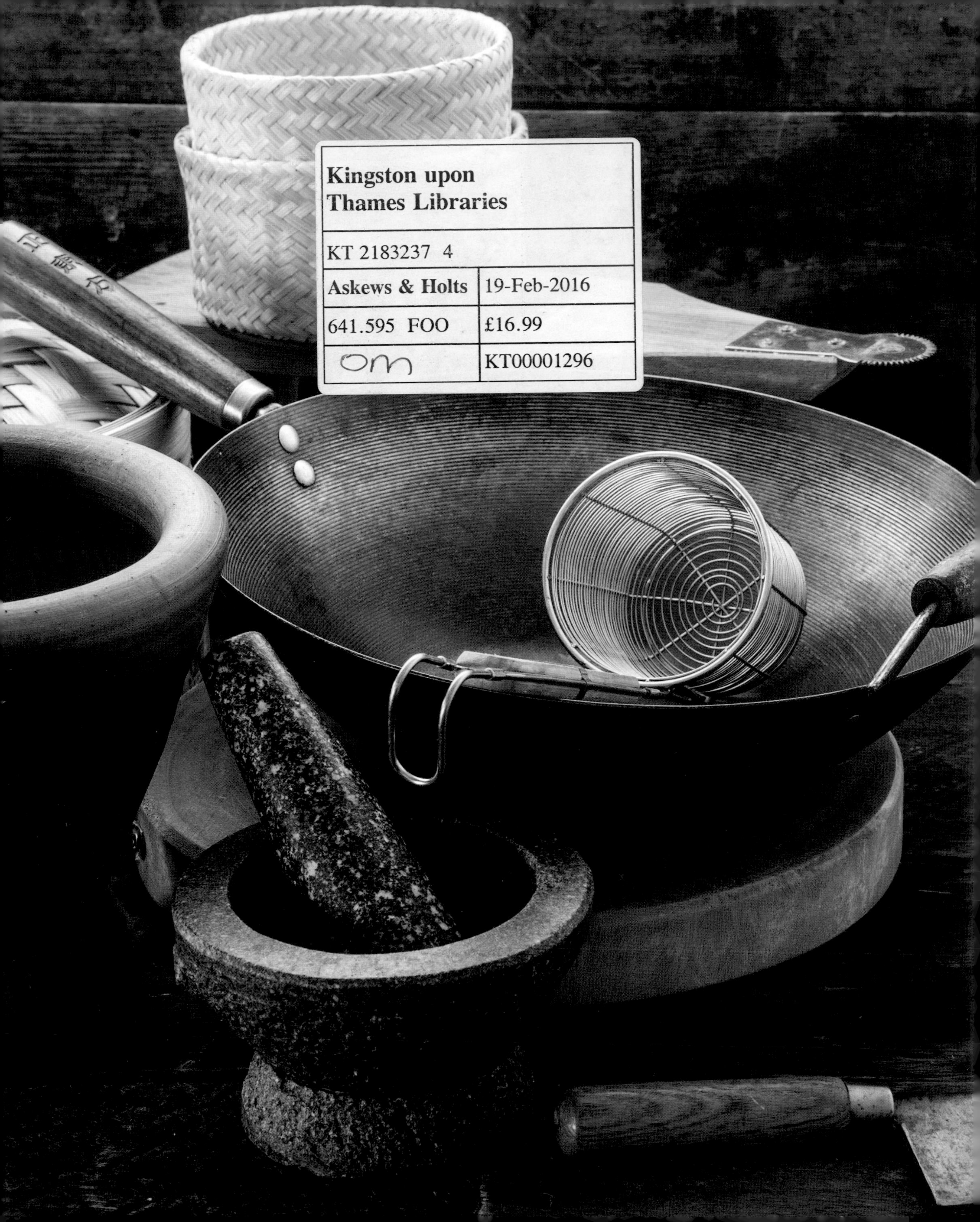

Content

Introduction

My first experience of Thailand was something I will never forget. I was on a four-week holiday with my family. It was so different from my life back home. For a start, the roads were chaos. I remember travelling down the freeway, cars and trucks flying past, whole families riding on one small scooter with no helmets, cars and trucks overloaded with fruit, vegetables and other produce, no seatbelts or baby capsules for protection. It was a bit of a mind spin really. As a chef, I was surprised at the lack of food safety—whole pig carcases left out in the hot, humid weather with hundreds of flies crawling all over them; street food stalls with very limited equipment and seemingly no regulation for food preparation. It was quite shocking for me and very different from what I was used to working as a chef in Australia.

At the time, I was an open-minded, young person and I thought and open to new and exciting experiences. The culture shock that is Thailand surprised me. Here I was, a white guy who thought I knew it all. How wrong I was. Fortunately, my Thai wife, Sirawan, soon set me straight explaining the customs and the way of life of Thai people. I have since fallen in love with the country, embraced the food and the Thai way of life.

Since that first trip, I've been back many times. From a foodie's perspective, I buy whatever I want from street stall vendors. I have included some of these recipes in this book because I've come to love Thai street food. It's a way of life for Thai people that is experienced on the streets of cities and towns throughout Thailand. Walking the streets of Thailand, the delicious smells waft through the air; the smell of savory curries, grilled chicken and salted snakefish, the sweet smell of grilled banana and coconut desserts that often have been prepared only minutes before—you want to consume all that you see and smell.

The street stalls with exotic, enticing scents and smells, and the array of vendors is truly a sight to behold—a chef's paradise and seriously the best experience you could possible imagine.

Thai food today comes from a complex history with countries in close proximity to Thailand that have contributed to what we know as Thai food. In this book, I explore some of the history and culture of Thailand to show how Thai cuisine has evolved. You can read about the history and culture if you're interested or go straight to the recipes and start cooking.

Thailand is a magical country with the best food in the world, the best culture and the happiest people. I am in love with everything Thai and it's not just me. Thailand is recognized throughout the world as a number one holiday destination and their cuisine is recognized as the most popular Asian cuisine in the world, exported to just about every country.

I wrote *Thai Food Sensation* to share what I have been given from my Thai family and friends who have taught me so much about the history, the culture, the cuisine, and most importantly, about the people of Thailand. I hope you to can experience the wonder of Thailand and the delights of Thai cooking within these pages.

About Thailand

Thailand is a country in south-eastern Asia. Situated below China, and just above Malaysia, it also has borders with Cambodia, Lao and Burma.

It is the 20th largest country in the world with almost 70 million people who call Thailand home. Bangkok is the capital; the political, commercial and industrial hub of the country.

Most people will have heard of Phuket because of its reputation as a tourist mecca. It is located on an island just off the coast on the western side of Thailand. Other major cities include Chiang Mai in the north and Pattaya, located some 99 miles (160 kilometres) from Bangkok on the Gulf of Thailand.

Culturally, Thailand has four distinct regions—and 76 provinces—all with their own distinct history, geography, culture and cuisine. The climate also varies from region to region from very lush and tropical with fertile soils to dry and arid with poor soils. Because of such variations, the produce from each region varies too.

Produce from the south includes seafood, nuts and coconuts. From the central plains come rice, herbs and fruit, and from the north-east and north, sticky rice, meats and fermented foods.

The main religion of Thailand is Buddhism with over 97 per cent of population being Buddhist. In every province, there are beautiful Buddhist temples and even in the most inaccessible places, on mountain tops and deep with the thickest jungles, Buddhist temples can be found.

Food is central to Thai culture with language and expressions specifically related to the eating of food. In many countries, a greeting is "How are you today?" The Thai greeting is a bit different. They say to their friends "Have you eaten yet?"—an invitation to sit and dine together. To bring rice or to offer a bowl of rice is a sign of respect and a sign of friendship. Everything about the culture of Thailand revolves around food and of eating it.

Regions of Thailand

From the jungle-covered mountain ranges in the north, the tradition and culture of the north-east, to the central region known as Thailand's rice bowl, and the tropical landscape of the south, Thailand has a rich diversity.

The four main regions are:

The North—*Park Neua*

North East—*Isaan*

The Central Plains—*Park Glang*

The South—*Pak Dtay*

The North—Park Neua

The northern region is a mountainous terrain covered with evergreen forests, that once contained wild animals including monkeys, deer, cattle, bears and tigers. The forest is lined with deep valleys, rivers and lakes.

All through *Park Neua*, there are ancient cities and crumbling temples from the Sukhothai Era.

The northern cuisine has been influenced by surrounding countries, Burma and India further west, Laos to the north-east and China further north.

Such influences have produced a diet with a much higher fat content than southern regions. Spices are used heavily with the main flavors being salty and spicy.

The region is home to the famous *Larb*. A salad made with any type of protein, especially pork or chicken, this dish uses an elaborate mix of dried spices as flavoring and seasoning including ingredients such as cumin, cloves, long pepper, star anise and cinnamon amongst others.

Some favorite dishes from the region

Spicy Northern Sausage—Sai Ooua

This is a Chiang Mai Sausage basically made from pork and spices. Grilled over coals and served with sticky rice and fresh vegetables with a handful of fresh chilies.

Ground Pork Dip—Naam Prik Ong

Naam Prik Ong is a fermented pork dip served with fresh vegetables and roti. It is extremely tasty.

North East—Isaan

Isaan is the largest region of Thailand covering more then one third of Thailand.

It is bordered by Laos to the north and Cambodia to the south-east—separated by the largest river in the region, the Mekong River (also known as the MeKong River).

Isaan is a very dry and harsh region. With very little rainfall during the year, it is very difficult to farm as very little can be grown in the barren, clay-like soil. During the summer, the land is extremely dry leaving the earth cracked and killing almost any plant or vegetation. When the monsoon rains come, the once dry landscape turns into a flooded wetland. Despite the adverse conditions, most of the population are farmers who subsist on what they can.

Because of the harsh conditions, *Isaan* is the poorest region in the country. This may account for the fact that *Isaan* people will eat anything that is a source of food: grasshoppers, bugs, field rats, snakes and lizards. *Isaan* people do not waste any part of the animal and when making a dish the *Isaan* people will chop the whole animal—bones and all. The cooks in *Isaan* are some of the best in Thailand—with very little, they create mouth-watering dishes with heat and balance.

Some Favorite Dishes from the Region

Green Papaya Salad—Som Dtam

The most popular Isaan dish is this spicy green papaya salad.

Ingredients can include garlic, chili, snake bean, lime juice, fish sauce, palm sugar, cherry tomatoes, peanuts, black salted crab, fermented anchovies, Thai olives, pork skin, bean sprouts, Thai eggplant and dried shrimp to name just a few!.

Grilled Chicken—Gai Ping or Yang

Most often this dish is grilled on coals on the side of the road at street food stalls or at markets. It is served with a spicy *Nahm Jim* sauce.

Grilled Pork—Moo Ping or Yang

This street snack is marinated with oyster sauce and sugar before being grilled on the coals. It is served with a handful of different sauces and mostly served with sticky rice.

The Central Plains—Park Glang

The Central Plains as the name suggests is made up of vast agricultural lands. With highly fertile soil and a consistent climate, the region produces the bulk of the country's food.

The Chao Phraya River and almost every river in Thailand meet here to create the Cho Phrya basin which allows the central plains to be well watered, the centre of Thailand's rice industries with rice fields as far as the eye can see.

This region is the most populated region in Thailand having been permanently settled for more then 2,500 years. This region is filled with old kingdoms and ruins from the oldest eras of Thailand.

The cuisine is complex and reflects the ancient history that once was, the palace is a large influence in the cuisine today being the home land of the beautiful fruit and vegetable carvings that are found all over Thailand. The Central Plains have been Thailand's political heartland for such a long time with the Central Plains cuisine being highly mixed with other Nationalities cuisines and cooking methods. Street food is one big part of this regions cuisine being it noodles to stir-fries, soups, salads and fried food.

Some Favorite Dishes from the Region

Fish Pate—Ho Mok Pla

This fish pate recipe resembles a soufflé-style of fish, mixed spices, coconut milk and egg all steamed in a banana leaf cup and topped with coconut cream before serving.

Green Curry—Kaeng Khiao Wan

This green curry is one of the spiciest of curries, made with fresh green chilies, Galangal and other amazing ingredients flavored with coconut cream and milk. It can be cooked with beef, pork, chicken and seafood.

Red Curry—Prik Gaeng Ped
This red curry is similar to green curry with a few differences. It's made with dried long red chilies, Galangal and lemongrass and with a range of different spices from the green curry.

Hot and Sour Soup—Thom Yum

Hot and sour soup is Thailand's most known soup—hot from chilies and sour from lime juice—it has a peppery flavor from the young galangal and a freshness from the lemongrass.

Hot and Sour Coconut Soup—Thom Kha

This hot and sour coconut soup is much like Thom Yum—the only difference is that Tom Kha has the added ingredients of coconut milk and a little coconut cream.

The South—Pak Dtay

The south of Thailand with its vast beaches, tropical climate and lush vegetation is a veritable paradise.

The region, on the narrow Malay Peninsula, has an abundance of seafood including lobster, king shrimp (prawns), clams, mussels, scallops, abalone, crabs, fish, cuttlefish, squid and shrimp. The seafood is added to curies or salads; the cuttlefish is dried; the shrimp used to make fermented fish paste and sauces.

The cuisine of the south is mostly flavored heavily with turmeric and other spices. Thai chili is used dried or fresh in almost every dish; coconut cream and milk are favored in most dishes and Muslim cooking influences also impact on the cuisine.

The curries found in this area are full of flavor and color—red, green and yellow curries can be found, along with Jungle curries and the famous Massaman curry is home to this region.

Some Favorite Dishes from the Region

Indian Muslim-style Curry—Kaeng Massaman

By far the most famous curry in Thailand, this Indian-style curry is made of roasted spices then cooked with beef or lamb and garnished with peanuts.

Vegetable Curry—Kaeng Tai Pla

A thick, sour, vegetable curry made with turmeric and shrimp paste contains fish innards, bamboo shoots and eggplant.

Satay

This is by far the most popular street snack—satay chicken or pork grilled on a low heat, served with cucumber dressing or just its own satay sauce of peanuts, turmeric and other herbs.

History of Thailand

Sukhothai Era

The very first Kingdom in Thailand, founded in 1238, was called Sukhothai, meaning the dawn of happiness.

The Kingdom of Sukhothai was a very beautiful city, with a backdrop of mountains and thick evergreen vegetation with huge carved stone imagines of the Lord Buddha. The Sukhothai Era was the foundation of Siam, where the first Thai alphabet was created, creating the name "Golden Age". The first King of Sukhothai was named King Pho Khun, the creator of Siam. The Thai cuisine and cooking styles back in the Sukhothai Era were mostly grilling and cooking directly on wood coals. Ingredients were hard to obtain and mostly fish, wild boar and field rats where eaten.

In the Sukhothai period, there were no chilies or other ingredients that are used in Thai cooking today. These ingredients only came to Thailand in the Ayutthaya Era some 100 years later.

The cuisine of the Sukhothai Era was heavily salted, like most countries of this period. Salt was used as a preservative by rubbing the meat or fish with salt then covering with a cloth or leaving to dry in the sun. Seafood was salted and sun dried, extending the life of the food for months. Wild herbs would have been pounded together with fermented fish and eaten with rice or fresh vegetables.

Traces of the kingdom of Sukhothai can be found today in the ruins that remain near Myanmar on the Malay Peninsula.

Ayutthaya Era

Around 1350, a new kingdom was created. Ayutthaya arose to the south of Sukhothai and, over the next four centuries, grew to become the wealthiest and most powerful kingdom in all south-east Asia. Under the command of King Uthong Ramathibodi, the founder of Ayutthaya, the kingdom grew into the largest kingdom in the world with a population of over one million.

The size and scale of Ayutthaya was considered huge for the period—many neighboring enemies feared the strength and the power of the kingdom.

In the late 1500s, the Portuguese discovered the "New World" which for Siam was the start of a culinary revolution.

The Portuguese people where the first European country to make contact with the Kingdom of Siam, introducing to the Siam people different ingredients that they had never seen before Including chilies, tomatoes, potatoes, eggplants and many herbs.

The Portuguese influences on Thai culture and food included the introduction of cooking utensils that the Thai people use today.

From this time on, many countries including China and India starting to trade with the Kingdom of Siam, giving the Siamese people an ever-expanding list of ingredients and cooking methods to enhance their cuisine. Dishes such as curries—including the Massaman curry—noodle soups and dishes and stir-fries were introduced during this period. The Ayutthaya Era was the most revolutionizing era in Thai Cuisine.

Although the Ayutthaya Kingdom was powerful, their biggest enemy was Burma. The Burmese invaded Siam a number of times with their goal firmly on Ayutthaya. In 1767, Ayutthaya fell to the invading Burmese army after a prolonged war that destroyed much of the national treasures. The few remaining buildings from the time of the Kingdom of Ayutthaya, crumbling but still beautiful, can be seen in the city.

Rattanakosin

After the Ayutthaya ransacking, the Burmese army retreated back to Burma due to an invasion by the Chinese.

There were a few different Kings after the fall of Ayutthaya with the main King being Rama I, who created the Rattanakosin era of peace and prosperity. King Rama I, II and III were very big believers in expansion and trade was there main focus and effects.

The Chinese came to Thailand by the hundreds to work in the newly-developed sugar cane factories that gave the Chinese an opportunity to earn a reasonable income. While working in the factories, many Chinese cooks and chefs shared their cooking methods such as steaming, wok frying and braising, and sharing new ingredients such as fresh noodles, duck eggs, vegetables and different cuts of meat. The Chinese brought with them the skills for making beef noodle soups, congee and so many other dishes we all love today. The Chinese also brought with them woks and pans.

The Thai cuisine today is built from the fusion of many different cuisines—the different flavors, textures, methods and cooking styles have blended over thousands of years to create a master cuisine of balance and harmony.

Religion of Thailand

Thailand is a very spiritual country, founded on the principles of Indian Buddhism. Buddhism is everything to Thai people who live and breath the Buddhist way of life. Monks are present from early mornings to late evenings, wandering, mediating and giving blessings to the people.

The Royal Family of Thailand must be of the Buddhist faith, uphold Buddhist laws, and unite the people under the Buddhism religion.

Buddhism teaches its followers to harness one's thoughts and actions and, by doing so, to find peace and healing from suffering.

In every province of Thailand there are beautiful temples—some can be found on the highest mountains or in the thickest jungles.

Buddhists must obey the five principles.

> One shall not harm or kill any living being or animal.
>
> One shall not steal.
>
> One shall not lie or gossip.
>
> One shall not engage in sexual misconduct.
>
> One shall not drink alcohol or take drugs.

The most respectful way to present your self to the Lord Buddha is by:

> wearing long clothing that are not to revealing
>
> not touching or kissing your loved ones in public
>
> taking your shoes off before entering a temple or home.

If you are visiting Thailand, there are some customs to follow when visiting temples.

Before entering the temple, you donate money to receive flowers, incense and gold leaf, then slowly walk to the Buddha and once below the Buddha, kneel then slowly bow your head with your hands together resting near your chest. Bow your head to the ground three times, opening your palm to the ground. pray to the Lord Buddha and then bow three times again. Give the flowers to the Buddha and light the incense. Place the gold leaf over the Buddha, bowing while standing.

The Thai people will embrace you and love you when you show them respect, and more importantly if you show respect to the Lord Buddha by doing a few simple steps. This does not mean you have to bow or pray if you are not Buddhist. Simply removing your shoes would be respectful enough.

Thai Cooking

If you want to get the flavors of authentic Thai cooking, you do need to have some of the main ingredients. It's a small investment for a huge reward and the good news is that many of the ingredients listed last a very long time.

Essential Ingredients

Bay Leaves
Bentel Leaves
Black Peppercorn
Cardamom pods
Cassia Bark
Cashew Nuts
Chili Flakes
Cilantro (Coriander) Seeds
Cloves
Coconut Cream
Coconut Milk
Condensed Milk
Crab Paste
Cumin Seeds

Dried Galangal
Dried Long Red Chilies
Dried Shrimp
Durian or Jackfruit
Fennel Seeds
Fish Sauce
Gapi (shrimp paste)
Grachai
Ground Roasted Rice
Jasmine Rice*
Light Soy Sauce
Macadamia Nuts
Nutmeg
Oyster Sauce

Palm Sugar
Peanuts
Pickled Ginger
Rice Flour
Salt
Salted Black Crab
Star Anise
Tamarind Pulp and Puree
Tapioca
Tempura Flour
Thai Olives
White Peppercorn

Jasmine rice has a high GI rating (glycaemic Index). For diabetics, substitute with a low GI rice such as Basmati, Mahatma or wild rice.

Fresh Ingredients

Cilantro (coriander)
Turmeric
Galangal
Garlic

Kaffir Lime Leaves
Kaffir Limes
Lemon Grass
Long Green Chilies

Long Red Chilies
Thai Basil
Thai Chilies
Thai Shallots

You can find most, if not all, of these ingredients in any good Asian supermarket. Also, many specialist food shops stock more Asian cooking ingredients.

Essential Equipment and Utensils

The most important utensil in a Thai kitchen is the granite mortar and pestle, followed closely by the terracotta mortar and wooden pestle. I find the best size to work with is a 9 inch (23 cm) mortar. The pestle comes with it.

What You Need

The following list shows some of the equipment and utensils that will make cooking Thai food that much easier.

Cast Iron Pans	Papaya Grater & Peeler	Sticky Rice Boiler
Coal Grill	Pastry Brush	Sticky Rice Steamer
Coconut Juicer	Rice Cooker	Strainer
Coconut Shredder	Saucepans	Terracotta Mortar & Pestle
Gloves	Scales	Tongs
Granite Mortar & Pestle	Sifter	Woks and Pots
Ladles	Spice Grinder	Wooden Skewers

Mortar and Pestle

Of all the equipment in the list, having the right mortar and pestle, is the most important.

When buying a mortar and pestle (either granite or terracotta), make sure they are large enough to make the pounding process easier and faster.

Why two mortars? The granite mortar is designed to pound curry pastes, roasted spices and fresh meats; the terracotta mortar is design to pound ingredients for salads only.

The Importance of Rice

Rice is the fundamental ingredient of many cuisines in south-east Asian countries including Thailand.

While rice was the staple of all dishes in the past, the affordability of meats and other produce has seen a change so that rice is becoming more a side dish than the main dish. Nevertheless, rice is still very important for Thai people.

There are two main types of rice eaten in Thailand. The first is jasmine rice, *Kaao Hom Mali* or *Kaao Suuai* which means beautiful rice.

The second rice is sticky rice, *Kaao Niiao*, which is eaten with grilled meats and salads but can be eaten with any dish if desired. Sticky rice has a higher content of starch and is cooked by steaming in a bamboo steamer.

Jasmine Rice—Kaao Hom Mali

Throughout Thailand, jasmine rice is the first choice of rice—and the most important aspect of Thai cuisine. There are a number of different types of jasmine rice that can be seen at the markets. Each rice is valued for a different reason; new-crop rice is young and fresh with more moisture and fragrance. Rice that is a year old or more is cheaper than fresh jasmine rice.

Sticky Rice—Kaao Niiao

The rice of the north and north-east regions of Thailand is *Kaao Niiao*. Before heading to bed, a bowl of *Kaao Niiao* would be covered with water and soaked overnight ready to be steamed first thing in the morning. A typical expression is, "A day without sticky rice is a day without water".

This rice is steamed in a bamboo basket over rapidly boiling water and then packed into bamboo boxes called *Gradtip Kaao*. A strong string attached from side to side makes it easy to carry on the back or over the shoulder. Farmers can be seen riding their motorbikes with their *Gradtip Kaao* slung over their shoulders ready to be eaten later in the day. The baskets are a wonderful portable carryall that keeps the rice warm and fresh.

Sticky rice is different to jasmine rice in that it has more starch —known as amylopectin and amylose starches. Once cooked, it comes out in a large clump that is somewhat chewy to eat. To eat sticky rice, pinch off small bite-sized piece. Roll it into a ball and dip into a relish or *Nahm Jim*. Alternatively, the rice ball can be flattened using the fingers and then used to shovel food from the plate.

Thai Grilling

The grill is an essential cooking item that has been with the Thai culture for decades. Everywhere you go in Thailand, the grill is used to cook main dishes (or to cook ingredients that are then added to pastes and soups). There are a number of different grilling methods.

Grilling—Ping

This is grilling over low coals until the food is cooked to golden or slightly toasted. It is excellent for dried squid that is placed onto the coals to release the tastes and oils from the squid.

Grilling—Yang

This is grilling over a low heat for a long time, as in grilled pork neck. It is used for cooking large pieces of meat. The slowness allows the meat to stay tender and also creates a smoky taste.

Chargrilling—Pao

Chargrilling, or charbroiling, is to cook over a high heat to blacken the skin—for example, bell peppers (capsicum) being chargrilled to remove the skin. Charring a vegetable develops a rich smokiness to the meat.

Dry Grilling—Siap

Meats and other ingredients are skewered then dried in the sun before being grilled—similar to salted marinated beef that is left in the sun for a day before being grilled or deep fried.

Bamboo Grilling—Larm

One of the oldest forms of grilling is to fill hollowed bamboo with sticky rice and black beans or vegetables that are filled with coconut cream or milk sugar sauce flavored with pandan leaf. These are grilled over embers so that the outer bamboo becomes blackened while the inside, the result is a smoky silky smooth creamy blend.

The advantage of using a coal grill is that it recreates the true taste and texture of Thai grilling that a gas or electric grill can't achieve.

Buying A Grill

Choosing the right grill can be a difficult choice as there are so many to choose from. Consider choosing a single plate grill that has weight and length as these are cheap and efficient. A gas barbecue grill is an option as is any manufactured pit and charcoal smoker.

Basic Thai Recipes

Thai food has many side dishes to go with a main dish—they are essential to Thai cooking and the way that the Thai people create a balance between flavors of sweet, sour, salty and spicy. They are the essentials; without them, it's not really Thai cooking.

The basics are primarily garnishes, such as shrimp floss and garlic oil. In relishes and dipping sauces, you'll find such favorites as sweet chili sauce.

Curry pastes and stocks include all the most popular Thai curry pastes and stocks. A Thai curry would not be a Thai curry without the magical pastes that have come to represent the best flavors in Thai cuisine.

THE BASICS

Adjard Syrup

500 ml (16 fl oz) rice vinegar
450 g (14½ oz) castor sugar

In a saucepan, add the sugar and the vinegar. Dissolve the sugar and simmer for 5 minutes.

Cool completely. Store in the refrigerator for up to 3 months.

Boiled Salted Duck Egg

1 duck egg
water

Cover the duck egg with cold water. Bring to the boil. Simmer for 10 minutes.

Chicken Wings, deboned

The simple way is to ask your local butcher to debone the wings. If you need to do this yourself, take the wing in your non-knife hand. Using a sharp boning knife, cut around the top of the chicken wing removing the flesh from the bone.

Use your knife to scrape outwards from the bone to remove all of the flesh. Use your hand and pull the flesh down until you reach the knuckle. The knuckle is the hardest part of the boning process. Slowly and carefully cut around the knuckle being careful not to cut the skin. Slowly move the flesh form the knuckle bone. Once the flesh has been removed, place your finger between the two winglet bones and pull the flesh downwards. Pinch the flesh on the outer bones and in a fast motion pull the flesh downwards again. Remove the two bones by simply turning the bones until they pop out.

Chili Flakes

125 g (4 oz) roasted or fried chilies (page 26)

Use a spice grinder or mortar and pestle to grind to a fine consistency.

Keep in an airtight container.

Chilies, Fried

250 g (8 oz) dried long red chilies
500 ml (16 fl oz) rice oil

Heat the oil in a frypan then add the chilies.

Fry for 40 seconds or until dark. Strain and place on a paper towel.

Chili Oil

500 ml (16 fl oz) rice oil
14 dried roasted chilies
4 Thai bird's eye chilies

2 garlic cloves
2 slices galangal

Pound chilies, garlic and galangal to a paste using a mortar and pestle.

Add oil to a frypan then add paste and simmer on a low heat for 30 minutes.

Allow to stand overnight. Strain and store in a glass airtight container.

Chilies, Roasted

250 g (8 oz) dried long red chilies
pinch of salt

Place the chilies on a baking tray. Sprinkle with salt.

Roast for 35 minutes or until the chilies darken. Turn the chilies over now and then.

Note: Having the oven exhaust fan on during the cooking will help prevent the smell of the chilies permeating the kitchen.

Fried Garlic

125 g (4 oz) garlic, sliced finely
1 L (35 fl oz) rice oil

Heat the oil in a large wok. Place the tip of a chop stick into the oil to check the heat. When small bubbles form around the chop stick, the oil is ready.

Add the sliced garlic. Simmer until golden, strain then place on paper towel. Cool and keep in airtight container for up to one week in a cool, dry place.

Fried Shallots

125 g (4 oz) shallots
1 L (35 fl oz) rice oil

Heat the oil in a large wok. Place the tip of a chop stick into the oil to check the heat. When small bubbles form around the chop stick, the oil is ready.

Add the sliced shallots. Simmer until golden. Strain and place on a paper towel. Cool and keep in airtight container for up to one week in a cool, dry place.

Garlic Oil

20 garlic cloves, chopped
250 ml (8 fl oz) rice oil

Place the oil into a saucepan over a low heat. Add the garlic cloves and allow the oil to come to a light simmer. Turn off the heat and allow to cool completely in the pan. Place into a container and allow to infuse for up to 10 hours before using. This oil will keep up to four weeks.

Ground Rice Powder

200 g (7 oz) raw glutinous rice (sticky rice)
3 kaffir lime leaves
2 slices galangal
½ lemongrass, purple part only sliced finely

Place ingredients in a cast iron pan. Cook until the rice is dark brown to an almost burnt. Keep moving the pan during the cooking; the rice does not take long to color. Allow to cool completely. Grind or pound to a semi-fine powder. Store in an airtight container.

Oyster Omelet

4 free range eggs
2 garlic cloves
4 fresh oysters, de-shelled
1 teaspoon fish sauce
1 teaspoon oil, for frying

Place all the ingredients into a bowl except the oil. Heat the oil in a frypan or omelet pan and bring to a medium heat. Pour the mixture into the pan. Allow the bottom to golden before gently flipping the omelet over. Cook until golden on each side.

Palm Sugar Caramel

330 g (11 oz) palm sugar
125 ml (4 fl oz) water

Add the palm sugar and water to a saucepan. Cook until it forms a light caramel, approximately 5 to 10 minutes. It will have a bubbly foam on the top that indicates the sugar is caramelizing.

Run some cold water into the sink. Make sure it is not too deep to allow any water to come into contact with the caramel. When the caramel is ready, place the bottom of the saucepan into the sink. Strain and place into an airtight container. It will keep in the refrigerator up to 4 weeks

Pandan Custard

625 ml (20 fl oz) coconut cream
375 ml (12 fl oz) milk
2 egg yolks
250 g (8 oz) white sugar
3 tablespoons tapioca flour
2 tablespoons cornstarch (cornflour)
6 tablespoons pandanus paste
pinch of salt

Add the coconut cream and milk to a saucepan and bring to the boil. Mix the egg yolks, sugar and flours together in a bowl. When the coconut milk is about to come to the boil, add half to the egg mixture in the bowl mixing well. Once the remaining milk comes to the boil, pour the egg mixture into the saucepan. Whisk until the mixture is cooked and thick.

Transfer the custard into a clean bowl. Add the pandanus paste and the salt. Cool to room temperature. If the mixture is too thick once cooled add a small amount of coconut cream or water.

Pickled Cucumber

200 g (7 oz) castor sugar
750 ml (24 fl oz) white vinegar
125 g (4 oz) roasted peanuts, crushed
2 baby cucumbers, de-seeded and diced
1 long red chili, sliced
3 cilantro roots, chopped
1 small clove garlic, chopped
pinch of salt
1 handful cilantro leaves
½ handful mint leaves

Bring the vinegar and the sugar to the boil in a saucepan. Take off the heat and allow too cool to room temperature. Add other ingredients once the liquid has cooled.

Roasted Nuts

When roasting nuts, keep in mind that they will keep cooking as they cool. It is best to cook until just golden then remove as quickly as possible from the hot oil.

125 g (4 oz) blanched peanuts
500 ml (16 fl oz) oil

Blanch the nuts by placing them in a frypan of boiling water. Boil for 1 minute. Drain immediately and rinse under cold water to prevent further cooking. Place onto a paper towel. Remove the skin on nuts such as almonds. Place the nuts on a tray in the oven without heat overnight.

Heat the oil in a saucepan and deep fry the nuts until golden. Remove and drain on paper towels to allow to cool completely before pounding or serving.

Roti

375 g (12 oz) all-purpose (plain) flour
250 ml (8 fl oz) water
1 teaspoon salt
1 tablespoon sugar
1 egg, lightly beaten
chives, optional

Combine flour and salt together in a bowl.

Mix the egg and water together then add to the flour mixture slowly. Mix until a dough is formed.

Kneed the dough for 10–15 minutes on a lightly floured board or benchtop to relax the gluten strains and to make the dough silky. Portion the dough into egg-sized balls then cover with a damp cloth for 3 hours or overnight.

Lightly flour a benchtop and use your fingers and palm to spread each ball into a flat round shape. Cover the other balls of dough with cling wrap while you work. If adding chives, before rolling, add a small amount to the top of the roti and roll over the top pushing the chives into the dough.

Pick up the dough and gently flick it down onto the bench (or use a rolling pin) to flatten as thin as possible.

Heat the pan on a medium heat and place a small amount of oil into the pan. Add the roti and cook until golden. Flip the roti, top with a nob of butter. Cook the other side until golden. Remove from the pan and slightly push the roti inwards to break it slightly. Chop the roti into large pieces and serve.

Note: The Thai method of whipping the dough on a bench takes years of practice so the easiest way to do this is by rolling the dough with a rolling pin.

Shrimp (Prawn) Floss

200 g (7 oz) dried Thai shrimp
500 ml (16 fl oz) rice oil

Heat the oil until just hot. Add the shrimp and fry until golden. Strain and place onto a paper towel. Cool completely. Use a spice grinder or mortar and pestle to grind shrimp to a fine powder.

Jasmine Rice, Steamed

This is the absorption method of cooking rice using an electric rice cooker. A deep saucepan with a tight-fitting lid will work as well. No only a rice cooker. I do not recommend any one cook rice in a saucepan. This recipe makes six cups.

425 g (15 oz) raw Thai jasmine rice
500 ml (16 fl oz) filtered water

Wash the rice three times before cooking. This will release the starch for a soft and fluffy result. To wash the rice, take the pot out of the rice cooker and add the rice. Fill to the top with water. Move the rice around with your hand, gently squeezing the rice. Pour the water out and repeat twice.

Once the water has been drained for the third time, place two cups of water into the pot. Place the pot back into the rice cooker and press "cook".

Electric rice cookers have markers to show the depth of water. However, to test yourself, once the water has been added, place your index finger on top of the rice. If the water just covers your finger, the depth is correct. Once the rice cooker has cooked the rice, take the lid off and carefully turn the rice with a spoon.

Note: I like my rice soft and a little dry so I place the lid back on and leave a small opening to release the steam. If you like your rice soft and a little wet, I suggest leaving the lid on tightly to keep the moisture inside. Keep any left over rice in the fridge for two days at the most. You can use the leftovers to make stir-fried rice.

The best way to refresh jasmine rice from the fridge is to add a small amount of water to the rice, then place it in the microwave for three to four minutes. The water will help to steam the rice and add moisture.

Sticky Rice—Kaao Niao

500 g (16 oz) Thai sticky rice (also called glutinous rice)
water

Put the sticky rice into a large bowl and cover with water. Soak overnight. The next day, strain any remaining water. Fill the bowl with cold water and gentle rub the rice to release any starch. Strain and repeat until the water is clear.

Fill a pot with water and bring to a rapid boil. Line the bamboo steamer with the muslin cloth and pour the rice into the bamboo steamer making sure to keep the rice on the muslin.

Carefully place the bamboo steamer over the boiling pot. Place a metal lid or a plate on the pot so there is no gaps for any steam to escape. Cook the rice for 10 minutes then turn the rice bundle over and cook for a further eight minutes.

The rice should be soft to the bite and somewhat clear; not hard nor mushy.

Once the rice is cooked, allow the rice to rest for 10 minutes then serve. The rice can be reheated by re-steaming for six minutes or microwave for one minute. Place a small amount of water on the rice before microwaving.

Sugar Syrup

500 ml (16 fl oz) water
375 g (12 oz) castor sugar

Bring the water and the sugar to the boil. Simmer for 30 minutes or until the liquid thickens slightly and the sugar is completely dissolved. Store in the refrigerator for up to 3 months.

Thom Yum Paste

9 long red chilies, sliced
3 Thai bird's eye chilies, sliced
5 kaffir lime leaves
pinch of salt
5 tablespoons lemongrass, sliced
10 slices galangal
7 cloves garlic, sliced
2 scallions (shallots), sliced
3 tablespoons cilantro root
1 teaspoon shrimp paste
4 tablespoons palm sugar
1 tablespoon fish sauce
4 tablespoons tamarind water
2 tablespoons oil

Pound garlic, cilantro root, galangal, lemongrass, chilies, kaffir lime and scallions to a paste. Heat the oil in a wok. Add the paste and fry on low heat for approximately 15 minutes. Allow to sweat off and build in color.

Add fish sauce, tamarind and palm sugar and simmer for 2 minutes or just before it becomes a jam consistency. Take off the heat. Cool completely. Store in an airtight container in the refrigerator for up to 1 month.

RELISHES AND
DIPPING SAUCES

Thai relishes and dipping sauces are the very soul of Thai cookery. Every Thai region has its own variations, many of which date back to the Sukhothai era, an era known for the flourishing nature of the Thai culture.

The discovery of palm sugar, coconuts, garlic, shallots, limes and herbs revolutionized the old fermented versions. The biggest change came with the introduction of chili.

Relishes add texture, taste, freshness and spiciness to a dish, without which the dish would have no body or soul.

Thai relishes vary greatly between regions. For example, in Bangkok palm sugar is used to create a relish, whereas in the north eastern regions of Thailand, the same sauce may be made using cane sugar or brown sugar (although sometimes palm sugar is also used).

SEAFOOD DIPPING SAUCE

NAHM JIM TALAY

Nahm Jim is Thai for dipping sauce. The foundation of a *Nahm Jim* is the combination of salty, sweet, spicy and sour. The main ingredients in *Nahm Jim* are garlic, fish sauce, chilies, sugar and lime juice. These are pounded together in a mortar and pestle then served as a side to a chosen dish.

Nahm Jim can be made with red chilies or green chilies or some of both. Making this sauce is a balancing act to get the flavors just right.

The sauce will keep for a few days but you may choose to throw out leftovers and making it fresh every time as it only takes five minutes to make. Although this *Nahm Jim* is called 'seafood', it goes well with any protein.

9 fresh Thai green chilies
9 fresh Thai red chilies
6 cloves garlic
4 cilantro roots
2 tablespoons cilantro leaves
4 tablespoons fish sauce
4 tablespoons lime juice
2 tablespoons palm sugar
pinch of salt

Place the chilies onto a tray and grill until the skins have blistered and are slightly blackened. Peel the skin off the chilies.

Using a mortar and pestle, pound the garlic, cilantro roots and palm sugar until it forms a fine paste. Add the chilies, and pound until very well mixed. Add in the fish sauce and lime juice and mix until the pasted is well blended.

Add the cilantro leaves and serve immediately.

ROAST TOMATO RELISH

JAEW MAKUEA TED

This relish is beautiful with any dish. Roasting the ingredients gives the relish a smoky flavor and adds so much richness to the relish. If you don't like the relish too hot, de-seed the chilies. This relish is commonly eaten with grilled meats, but can also be eaten with seafood.

This relish is rich, salty and spicy.

6 long red chilies
6 small Thai chilies
4 shallots roasted
6 garlic cloves roasted
2 whole tomatoes
4 cilantro roots
3 tablespoons fish sauce
1 tablespoon tamarind water
1 tablespoon lime juice
2 tablespoons palm sugar

Roast the chilies, shallots and garlic, on a tray in the oven or grill over coals until lightly blackened. Once you remove the chilies, shallots and garlic, roast the tomatoes on the grill separately.

Skin the tomatoes and peel the skin off the garlic.

Place the palm sugar into the mortar and mix until it forms a smooth paste. Add in the roasted ingredients and mix until it reaches a rough consistency.

Mix in the fresh cilantro roots, palm sugar, fish sauce, tamarind water and the lime juice and mix in well.

Serve with grilled meats or seafood and sticky rice.

ROAST BANANA PEPPER RELISH

NAHM PRIK NUM

This relish is by far one of my favorite Thai relishes as large banana peppers are full of flavor. It is very spicy and has a slightly fishy taste, which comes from from the shrimp paste and fermented anchovies. It is great served with grilled pork and grilled chicken cooked on the coals but any grilled meat or even seafood goes great with *Nahm Prik Num*. It is normally served with sticky rice and a side of fresh vegetables.

20 green banana peppers roasted and peel the skins
13 garlic cloves
6 Thai chilies
4 pieces cilantro root
1 tablespoon palm sugar
1 teaspoon fermented anchovies (optional)
1 tablespoon shrimp paste
2–3 tablespoons fish sauce
2–3 tablespoons lime juice

Grill the banana peppers over hot coals or roast in the oven. Place in a small bowl with cling wrap and allow to sit for 10 minutes—this will help remove the skin. Peel the peppers and set aside.

Add the garlic and chilies to a terracotta mortar and pound to a paste. Add the cilantro roots and palm sugar and pound some more.

Add the skinned peppers to the mortar with the anchovies and shrimp paste. Lightly bruise the peppers and anchovies so that the mixture stays chunky rather than a smooth paste.

Add the fish sauce and lime juice. Taste and season to your liking.

Serve in a side bowl with your choice of grilled meats or seafood and sticky rice.

DRY ROASTED CHILI SAUCE

NAHM PRIK JAEW

Nahm Jim Jaew is a really deep flavored sauce. The roasted chilies and sticky rice powder give the sauce an intense, smoky flavor that goes well with any grilled meat. The fresh herbs and shallots give freshness and texture.

2 tablespoons ground rice powder (page 28)
2 tablespoons chili flakes
3 fresh red chilies
1 clove garlic
4 pieces cilantro root
2 teaspoons palm sugar
2 tablespoons lime juice
2 tablespoons fish sauce
2 shallots
1 tablespoon cilantro leaves (optional)

Roast the rice into a cast iron pan. Slowly cook the rice until it's slightly burnt, then cool. Add to a granite mortar and pound to a fine powder. Set aside until needed.

Heat the cast iron pan to a high heat. Before adding the chili flakes, turn the exhaust fan on high and open the windows. Add the chili flakes and quickly toss until the oils and aroma are released, then transfer onto a plate to cool.

Pound together the fresh chilies, garlic and cilantro root in a terracotta mortar. Add the palm sugar, lime juice and fish sauce.

Slice the shallots and add to the mortar and then pound lightly to bruise. Once all the ingredients are combined, add chili flakes and the rice powder. Mix well.

The sauce should have a runny consistency and be a balance of salty, sour and spicy. You can add a tablespoon of cilantro leaves if desired.

Serve as a side. It is best not to store any leftovers as the sauce thickens due to the rice powder. and store any leftovers in a small glass airtight jar in the refrigerator.

TAMARIND CARAMEL

MAKHAM KHARA MEL

Tamarind caramel is a sweet and sour caramel that is mostly used on betel leaf and can also be eaten with pork neck.

4 tablespoons palm sugar
4 tablespoons tamarind water
1 lemongrass stalks, inner part, finely sliced
7 kaffir lime leaves, finely sliced
2 long chilies, de-seeded and finely diced
2 whole cilantro roots
1 lime juiced
2 tablespoons fish sauce

Heat the palm sugar in a cast iron pan over a slow flame until it caramelizes. Add the tamarind water gently. Stir slowly to avoid burning the caramel. Allow palm sugar and tamarind to simmer for three minutes.

While the caramel is simmering, in the terracotta mortar, bruise the lemongrass, kaffir lime leaves, chilies and cilantro root. Add this mixture to the tamarind caramel.

Using the back of a metal spoon, carefully press the ingredients to help release the oils and aroma. Turn the heat down and allow the caramel to thicken.

Once all the flavor has been released, sieve the caramel and discard the used ingredients. Add the fish sauce and lime juice to the caramel.

Allow to cool completely at room temperature.

Serve as a side and store any leftovers in a glass airtight container in the refrigerator.

CHILI JAM

NAHM PHRIK PAO

Chili jam is very universal. It can be used as a dip or as the basis of dishes and sauces. Best to make a batch and leave it in the refrigerator; it will keep for a few months. The jam should be slightly salty, sour and sweet.

1 L (16 fl oz) rice oil
6 shallots, sliced
250 g (8 oz) garlic, sliced
125 g (4 oz) dried shrimp
250 g (8 oz) long chilies, dried
1 tablespoon galangal
250 g (8 oz) palm sugar
125 ml (4 fl oz) tamarind water
125 ml (4 fl oz) fish sauce
250 g (8 oz) fresh long chilies, de-seeded
2 teaspoons shrimp paste

Heat the oil in a wok to a high temperature. Add the shallots and fry to a light golden color. Remove and strain. Starting with the garlic, then dried shrimp, dried and fresh chili and galangal, fry each ingredient separately and transfer each to a paper towel to drain.

Add all fried ingredients to a granite mortar and pound to a fine paste. Add the shrimp paste

Heat the wok to a high heat. Add a small amount of the oil that was used for deep frying. Once the oil is hot, add the paste and sweat off. Add the palm sugar, tamarind and the fish sauce. Simmer until the paste is thick and has a jam consistency.

Store in a glass airtight container in the refrigerator for up to three months.

TAMARIND WATER

NAHM MAKHAM

Tamarind water is used in many different dishes and sauces. It is best to make a batch and keep it in the refrigerator for up to 2 months.

1 packet whole tamarind
625 ml (20 fl oz) boiling water

Place the tamarind into a bowl. Pour boiling water over the top and allow to set for 30 minutes.

Use your hands to squeeze the pulp and seeds away from each other. Strain the mixture reserving the water for later use. Discard of the seeds and outer layer of the tamarind.

Store in a glass airtight container In the refrigerator for up to 3 months.

SWEET CHILI SAUCE

NAHM JIM KAI

This sauce goes well on all grilled food.

125 g (4 oz) sugar
125 ml (4 fl oz) Thai white vinegar
60 ml (2 fl oz) water
4 chilies, sliced
4 garlic cloves, chopped
1 teaspoon salt

Place the sugar, vinegar and the water together into a saucepan. Bring to a simmer and allow to simmer for 6 minutes.

Pound the chilies and the garlic to a course paste. Add to the saucepan and allow to cool completely.

Store in a glass airtight container in the refrigerator for up to 3 months.

SWEET TAMARIND DIPPING SAUCE

NAHM JIM GAI YANNG

This sauce is sweet and tangy with a good amount of heat. It is normally served with grilled chicken, *Gai Yaana Kamin* (page 96) and with sweet chili sauce, *Nahm Jim Kai*, (page 42) to provide a choice of dipping sauces.

3 tablespoons palm sugar
3 tablespoons tamarind paste
60 ml (2 fl oz) fish sauce
250 ml (8 fl oz) water
1 tablespoon chili powder

Add palm sugar, tamarind paste, fish sauce and water to a saucepan. Bring to the boil and then turn to a simmer. Allow to simmer for 5 minutes then take off the heat. Add the chili powder and allow to cool completely.

Store in a glass airtight container in the refrigerator for up to 3 months.

SOAKED CHILIES IN FISH SAUCE

PHRIK NAHM BPLAA

Phrik Nahm Bplaa is one of the most popular side dishes in the Thai kingdom. It is seen on all the street tables in little jars because it is used with so many Thai dishes.

7 green chilies, sliced
7 red chilies, sliced
125 ml (4 fl oz) fish sauce
4 garlic cloves, sliced finely

Combined the ingredients together and serve.

This will last for 2 days so it is best to make it fresh every time.

VINEGAR SOAKED CHILIES

PHRIK NAHM SOM

Phrik Nahm Som is always found next to *Phrik Nahm Bplaa*. They are like best buddies that go so well together and can be found in the Garnish & Sides on chosen dishes.

7 green chilies, sliced
7 red chilies, sliced
125 g (4 fl oz) Thai-brand white vinegar

Combined ingredients together. This will last for 2 days only. It is best to make it fresh every time.

SALTED PORK MINCE SIMMERED IN COCONUT CREAM

LON NAEM

Lon is an awesome relish dip that is sour, sweet and rich. Served with an arrangement of fresh vegetables that can be raw, steamed, boiled grilled or pickled. It can also be served with boiled duck or chicken eggs. It makes a wonderful starter to a meal and one that will impress your friends and family.

500 g (1 lb) pork mince
1 tablespoon salt
3 tablespoons pork fat or oil
4 shallots, sliced
3 garlic cloves, sliced
1 tablespoon cilantro root, chopped
500 ml (16 fl oz) coconut cream

500 ml (16 fl oz) coconut milk
3 tablespoons tamarind water
 (page 41)
1½ tablespoons pickled ginger,
 chopped
4 tablespoons fish sauce
90 g (3 oz) palm sugar

Garnish
1 long green chili, sliced
pinch fried shallots (page 27)
cilantro leaves, torn

Add the pork mince and salt to a bowl. Mix well. Allow to cure overnight in the refrigerator.

Heat a saucepan with the pork fat or oil. Add the shallots and garlic and sweat off. Add the cured pork and cook for 4 minutes or until most of the pork has been sealed (browned). Add the coconut cream and milk. Simmer for 15 minutes, then add the tamarind water, pickled ginger, cilantro root and palm sugar. Simmer for 10 minutes. Add the fish sauce slowly and taste as you go. There should be a balance of sour, sweet and salty. Reduce to a semi-thick relish consistency.

Serve in a bowl and top with garnish selection.

STOCKS AND PASTES

Stocks

Sa Dtok

A stock is enhanced with vegetables and bones such as chicken, duck, beef and pork bones. The bones of quails and rabbits can also be used. It is simmered over a long period of time to extract the entire tastes of each ingredient. Stocks are used mostly in soups and curries to add a depth of flavor.

Some tips for cooking stock

❉   Before cooking the bones, give them a wash and remove any fat so that the stock does not become too oily.

❉   A stock should never be stirred or moved. If stirred, the stock will became very cloudy.

❉   Allow the stock to reduce slowly as this prevents the proteins breaking apart and therefore creates a clear stock.

❉   When making a white stock base, chicken, fish or vegetable, do not use any green parts of vegetables as this will turn the stock to a gray color.

A main base for a Thai stock would consist of white cabbage, garlic, lemongrass, galangal, cilantro root, ginger, radish and white onion. The darker stocks such as beef and pork will have green vegetables, spices and char-grilled ingredients. Most stock recipes have instructions to fry off the bones before being added to the stock. Although this is true, I have also seen Thai cooks add uncooked bones to the stock without affecting the flavor.

For all stocks, during the reduction process, skim the surface, as this will prevent the stock becoming cloudy and bitter. Once the stock has reached the appropriate level of reduction, it should be sieved through muslin cloth so that it is completely clear.

A stock not only adds so much flavor, it's easy to make and can be stored in a freezer for months—so go nuts and make a huge amount then freeze it down.

Stocks are very simple to make and take very little time to prepare. There are two main stocks in Thai cuisine.

❉   Vegetable
❉   Chicken

Included in this section are also fish, pork and beef stocks as these are used in some Thai dishes.

CHICKEN STOCK

SA DTOK GAI

This stock is a great stock to make in large amounts and freeze in portions to use in recipes as required.

2 kg (4.4 lb) chicken bones
1 knob ginger, whole
3 garlic cloves, whole
½ cabbage, sliced
3 cilantro roots
1 stalk of celery, diced
1 carrot, diced
1 onion, diced

Wash the chicken bones and remove any fat. Break the bones to release the juices from the bones during the cooking period.

Add bones and vegetables to a large saucepan and cover with water. Simmer for 2 hours. Use a ladle to remove any fat or froth that comes to the top of the stock.

Drain the stock, strain through muslin, then freeze. Remove any fat that has congealed on the top. Use as required. The stock will last in the refrigerator up to 1 week. You can freeze it for up to 3 months.

VEGETABLE STOCK

SA DTOK PAK

This is a basic stock that can be used for any dish. I tend to use more vegetable stock than any other due to the richness of the ingredients and the availability to add more flavor to the stock for whatever dish I'm creating.

1 bunch celery, diced
2 onions, diced
2 garlic cloves, diced
6 carrots, diced
1 bunch cilantro root
1 white radish, diced
½ cabbage, shredded
6 L (12½ pints) water

Place all the vegetables in a large pot and add the water.

Cook for 1½ hours or until the vegetables are soft. While cooking, use a ladle to clean off any excess that may form on the top of the stock.

Strain the stock and squeeze the vegetables with a ladle to remove all the juices. Strain a second time. Use as required.

FISH STOCK

SA DTOK BPLAA

The secret to making fish stock is to not touch it while cooking. Do not move the fish around as this will separate the flesh from the bones and make your stock cloudy. The stock will last for 3 months in the freezer and a week in the refrigerator.

2 kg (4 lb) fish bones
1 celery stick
1 carrot, diced
2 cilantro roots
2 knobs ginger
1 tablespoon lemongrass, chopped
1 tablespoon fish sauce

Wash the fish bones and remove the skin and any fat. Add the fish, vegetables, herbs and fish sauce to a large saucepan and cover with water.

Simmer for 1 hour, then strain the stock twice through a sieve. Discard the bones and vegetables. Use as required.

PORK STOCK

SA DTOK MUU

This pork bones in this stock are already quite salty, so salt does not need to be added. This stock can be frozen for up to 3 months. It will last for a week in the refrigerator.

3 kg (6½ lb) pork bones
1 bunch cilantro
1 brown onion
1 garlic bulb
2 tablespoons soy sauce
1 lemongrass stalk
1 galangal
6 L (12½ pints) water

Place all the ingredients in a large pot with the water. Bring the pot to the boil, then simmer for 3 hours on a low flame. Skim the stock with a ladle to remove any fat from time to time.

Strain the stock then freeze. Remove any fat that has congealed on the top. Use as required.

BEEF STOCK

SA DTOK NEUA

Thai beef stock is more of a broth that is infused with spices and herbs. If you want a clear 'non-spicy' broth, do not add the spices. The chicken stock gives the broth a more complex overall taste.

5 L (10½ pints) chicken stock or water
2 kg (4 lb) oxtail or beef shin bones
1 garlic bulb, unpeeled
4 large onions, unpeeled
125 g (4 oz) ginger, peeled
1 bunch cilantro roots
1 tomato
8 whole cloves
5 whole star anise
2 cassia bark
1 tablespoon black pepper corns

Add the chicken stock or the water to a large pot. Wash the bones and then add to the liquid.

Grill the garlic and onion until their skins are blackened. Add the garlic and onion to the stock with all the other ingredients, except the dry spices (choves, star anise, cassia bark and pepper corns). Heat a dry cast iron pan. Add the spices separately on low heat and toss until they give off a rich aroma. Add spices to a mortar as they are cooked. When all have been added, pound to a fine powder.

Place into a muslin cloth and add to the stock. Simmer the stock for 4 hours until the flavor is rich. Strain the stock through muslin then freeze. Remove any fat that has congealed on the top. Use as required.

Pastes

Geng

Pastes are used to make Thai satays and Thai curries that can be mild and sweet, fiery hot and pungent, sour and bitter, or strong tasting and salty.

Every Thai family has their own recipes for curries and pastes that have been handed down through the generations. They will have secrets and stories behind them and instructions on how to incorporate every ingredient from chili to garpi.

Thai curries date back from the very beginning, from when the Thais migrated from the south of China. The old style curries were not as complex as there are today. Due to the revolution of the new world and trade ports being built, the Thais were able to develop their curries pastes by adding more herbs and vegetables. This resulted in a culinary revolution and made Thai curries as we know them today.

Curries in the Sukhuthai Era would have been mostly made with red shallots, white peppercorns, grachai and wild fish mixed together and then added to boiling water and finished with wild herbs and species.

Making a Curry Paste

To make a great curry paste, one must learn the technique and develop the patience to make a smooth and complete paste that is balanced and allows each ingredient to be tasted without one overpowering all the other tastes.

When starting a curry paste, make sure you have all the ingredients chopped or diced finely. This will make the process quicker and easier. The most important aspect of making a curry paste is to pound each ingredient to a fine paste before adding the next ingredient.

A curry paste should be made with a granite mortar and pestle which is a heavier and more coarse in texture allowing the ingredients to pound smoother.

Breakout box text: Although a food processor can be used, I would only used a food processor if in the restaurant or if making a high amount, as the texture and overall taste does differ from that of a mortar-made paste.

The way to make a curry paste smooth is to know the sequence of adding each ingredient and why each ingredient has a time and place within the curry paste. When adding ingredients to the mortar, the order is driest to wettest.

The dryer the ingredient, the less water content that ingredient has and the harder it is to pound. The younger and fresher the ingredient, the higher the water content and the easier it is to pound and incorporate.

Cooking the Paste

I have seen a number or different ways to cook a paste. There are cooks that will marinate their chosen meat with the paste then fry the paste and meat together. Some cooks will start with coconut cream and then add the paste, while others simply fry the paste in oil. All these different versions work—it's simply matter of preference.

The best way to learn how to make a paste is to practice and to learn when the next ingredient is to be added and also when the paste is finished. The smell, the texture and the look of the curry paste will tell you when it is ready—a skill only learnt through trial and error.

If the curry paste is pale, there could be a lack of chilies or an overload of other ingredients.

If the curry is lumpy and "sandy", this is due to not pounding the ingredients correctly.

Ingredients in a Paste

There are many ingredients that can be used to make a curry paste; each ingredient is just as important as the next. Here's a quick overview of the different ingredients used.

Chilies

There are many different chilies that can be used to make a paste for any of the curry-based dishes. For example, scud chilies are used in making jungle curry. Long dried red chilies are used in making red curry or *Thom Yum* pastes. Long green chilies are used in making green curries. The most used chilies would be the long red and long green ones as they have less heat in them. Smaller red chilies (bird's eye) are very hot so take care if using these.

When choosing a chili, it is important to understand what the chili will give you and the overall color and texture that chili will provide. When buying fresh long chilies I find the best to use are the semi-soft chilies. These chilies contain less water, their color is much darker than the freshest chilies and they are a lot easier to pound.

Dried red chilis need to be soak for 12 hours in cold water. If you are in a hurry, you can soak them in hot water for 15 minutes, but only use this method for emergencies. Once the chilies have soaked, they need to be drained and de-seeded.

In most cases, chilies will need to be de-seeded before being pounded. By cutting them into small pieces, the pounding process is quicker and easier. The amount of chili you use can be determined by your own heat preference. Do try to increase the heat level as Thai food is made to be spicy and punchy.

Salt

Salt is added to the chilies to help break them down and to act as an abrasive. It will also help in preserving the paste. Only a pinch is needed.

Lemongrass

Lemongrass is an amazing plant that is extremely versatile and used in many Thai dishes. It is used for its sour element and the unique taste, freshness and aroma it brings to a paste. Only use the purple inner part of the lemongrass—the outer layers are fibrous and are

very difficult to break down inside the paste. It is very important to slice the lemongrass very finely before adding to the chilies. This will allow the two ingredients to combine a lot easier and it will take less time to pound.

Galangal

Galangal is a part of the ginger family, called rhizome, that is used extensively in Thai cooking. Galangal brings a peppery taste to the paste and adds body. Galangal is considered the Yin, as it is a cooling rhizome. The best galangal to use for curry pastes is the dark reddish variety as these are more pungent. The best way to prepare the galangal is to remove the skin, then slice into very thin slices so that the pounding process is smoother.

Shallots

Shallots give the curry a sweet element. Slice the shallots very finely and then add to the mortar. Shallots can be added into the paste fresh or you can grill or deep fry first.

Garlic

Garlic is an essential ingredient that gives sharpness to the curry paste—too little and the curry paste will taste light; too much and the curry paste will be over pungent.

Lime Zest or Kaffir Lime

Lime zest is used in a curry to add a slight bitterness to the paste; it helps to bring out the intensity of other ingredients.

Shrimp Paste

Shrimp paste is used in curry paste to bring all the ingredients together; to enhance the other ingredients. Shrimp paste adds a richness to the curry and gives a slight saltiness. It can be roasted in the oven or a dry pan. To do this wrap the shrimp paste in silver foil and slowly roast or grill. Don't over cook, as this will make it very bitter.

Wild Ginger—Grachai

Grachai tastes very earthy. Grachai adds a peppery taste and is used mostly in seafood curries and dishes.

Cilantro (Coriander) Roots

Cilantro roots provide a fresh balance to a curry paste. Be careful as it can be a little over powering if you add too much.

Spices

Spices are used in many Thai dishes, mostly in the south where dishes are heavily seasoned with spices and chilies.

The most popular spices used in Thai cooking include the following.

* Peppercorn
* Cilantro seeds
* Cumin seeds

* Nutmeg
* Mace
* Cardamom
* Cassia
* Cloves
* Turmeric

The use of these ingredients vary from region to region. As stated previously, spices are found in southern Thailand curries and dishes.

Before adding spices to a curry paste or dish, they need to be added to a dry saucepan separately to allow the oils and fragrance to be released. Cool and pound into a fine powder then sieve before adding to the paste or dish.

Fresh Coconut Cream and Milk

Fresh coconut cream (and milk) is an amazing product that is creamy and full flavored. The best way to make a curry is to use fresh coconut cream and milk. It does however take time to make, but it is worth the effort.

There are a couple of different ways to make coconut cream and milk.

The first way is to use a coconut grater that will grate the inside of the coconut to a fine powder. Warm water is added to the powder and soaked for about 15 minutes. Then, using a muslin cloth, squeeze out the liquid, this is your first press coconut cream and thick milk. A second run can give you more liquid although this second press will be a lighter coconut milk.

The second way is to cut out the meat of the coconut and using a cold press juicer, juice the coconut. If using an electric cold press juicer, the time will fly past and you will be left with the very creamy coconut cream.

Cracking the Cream

To crack the coconut cream is the most important part when making a curry. Cracking simply means to split the solids from the fat.

Once the coconut cream has been cracked, then the paste can be added. This will give the curry a oily texture and will give a better texture.

If using tinned coconut cream or milk, this is not a problem. Tinned products have added stabilizers that do not allow them to crack. By adding a small amount of oil to the coconut cream, you will be able to have the same affect as fresh but the overall taste will be different.

Peanuts or Nuts

Adding peanuts or other nuts to a curry paste is a very important step. The best way is to break the nuts in half and then roast or deep fry them. Some Thai cooks blanch the peanuts or nuts in water first to allow them to be cooked through. However, the nuts do need to be cooked through completely before being added or pounded into the paste.

I find breaking the nuts in half, then frying or baking them works just as well. Make sure your nuts of choice are golden brown before adding or pounding, as this will make a huge difference to the overall appearance—too lightly toasted and the curry will look pale; too dark and the curry will taste bitter and be burnt.

When adding a nut paste to a curry paste, it is very important to pound the nuts to a very fine paste. Pound until smooth and an oily shine appears, then add to the paste or dish.

Red Curry Paste

This recipe is for a standard red curry. For some recipes, other ingredients are added such as duck curry.

16 long red chilies, dried
3 long chilies, fresh, chopped
3 tablespoons galangal, chopped
4 tablespoons lemongrass stalks, chopped
4 tablespoons red shallots, chopped
3 tablespoons garlic, chopped
3 tablespoons cilantro root, chopped
2 kaffir limes, zest only
1 tablespoon shrimp paste

Add ingredients to granite mortar and pound with a granite pestle until you have a smooth paste. See making a paste (page 56).

Green Curry Paste

This recipe is for a standard green curry. For some recipes, other ingredients are added. If you want a very green color to your curry, juice 5 to 6 silverbeet leaves in a cold press juicer and add to the paste.

12 long green chilies, de-seeded and chopped
1 large pinch of salt
2 Thai green chilies, chopped
2 tablespoons red shallots, chopped
½ tablespoon tumeric, chopped
2½ tablespoons lemongrass, chopped
1½ tablespoons galangal, chopped
2 tablespoons garlic, chopped
1 tablespoon kaffir lime zest
2 tablespoons cilantro root, washed and chopped
1 teaspoon white peppercorn, roasted and pounded
½ teaspoon cumin seeds, Roasted, pounded
½ teaspoon coriander seeds, roasted and pounded
2 cardamom pods, roasted and pounded
½ tablespoon garpi (shrimp paste), fresh or roasted

Add ingredients to a granite mortar and pound with a granite pestle to make a smooth paste. See making a paste (page 56).

Thai Food Sensation

Yellow Curry Paste

9 dried long red chilies, soaked,
    de-seeded and drained
pinch of salt
2 tablespoons galangal, chopped
1½ lemongrass stalks, chopped
2 kaffir lime leaves, sliced finely
1 teaspoon lime zest, chopped
2 large red shallots, grilled and chopped
6 garlic cloves, grilled
2 teaspoons cilantro root
1 teaspoon white pepper corn, and pounded
1 nutmeg, roasted and pounded
1 tablespoon cilantro seed, and pounded
6 tablespoons roasted nuts, pounded (page 29)
1 teaspoon shrimp paste

Add ingredients to a granite mortar and pound with a granite pestle until you have a smooth paste. See details about making a paste (page 56).

Mussaman Curry Paste

10 long dried red chilies, soaked, de-seeded, drained
large pinch of salt
1 tablespoon garlic, grilled
5 small shallots, grilled
1 tablespoon galangal, grilled
1 tablespoon lemongrass, sliced, grilled
2 tablespoon cilantro roots, grilled
1 teaspoon cumin seeds, roasted and pounded
1 tablespoon cilantro seed roasted and pounded
1 teaspoon white pepper corns, roasted and pounded
½ nutmeg, roasted and pounded
3 cardamom pods, roasted and pounded
2 bay leaves ground, roasted and pounded
4 cloves, roasted and pounded
1 cassia bark, roasted and pounded
125 g (4 oz) peanuts, roasted and pounded
1 tablespoon shrimp paste, fresh

Add ingredients to a granite mortar and pound with a granite pestle until you have a smooth paste. See details about making a paste (page 56).

Morning
Meals

The mornings in Thailand start very early with most people already awake and outside by 5 am —their roosters are their alarm clocks as almost every one has one.

The mornings in Thailand are very magical and very beautiful with the mist in the sky and the sun shining between the banana trees. The smell of smoke fills the air from grills being started for breakfast.

The markets are filling with the freshest produce; vegetables, meats and seafood as well as bunches of flowers that are made for the monks and put up for display.

People are setting up their morning stalls to make their earnings for the day. Older ladies can be seen carrying heavy pots, boxes of vegetables and cooked food heading to the markets.

On the streets the vendors are starting to simmer their pork stocks with a coal heat base, some using a wooden fire. The making of *Jok* and rice *congee* are on the go. Pork soft bones are being chopped and the fresh vegetables are washed and chopped. Chairs and tables are being set up. Relishes and vinegars are being placed onto the tables. Chinese bread is proving on wooden benches ready to be deep fried when the time is ready.

Thousand of motorbikes are flying past with children rushing off to school – first stopping to take a bag of food to eat later in the day. The Thai people don't eat breakfast like we westerners do. Thai people will eat what is leftover from the night before, or they buy already made food from the market or street stalls such as freshly deep fried bread, or pork floss with sticky rice. Sesame beef with sticky rice wrapped in banana leaves is also popular for breakfast. A very popular dish and my favorite breakfast meal is called *Jok*. This rice soup is so wonderful. It's the most for filling breakfast meal packed with flavor of pork, ginger, black pepper and soy sauce with a soft boiled egg on the top.

For anyone who loves coffee, the Thai coffee can be very strong and will wake the sleepiest person instantly. Having a Thai cup cake with a strong coffee is one of the best ways to awaken. The mornings of Thailand are so unique and very exciting. The mornings of Thailand are so uplifting that it would be difficult not to feel happy being apart of it all.

PORK PORRIDGE SOUP

MOO JOK

SERVES 4–5

This is a fast way to make *Jok*, which is one of the most popular dishes to start the day in Thailand.

Jok is served with a large choice of sides and flavorings. What makes Jok beautiful are the flavors and the textures. The pork and soft pork bones give an amazing body, The fresh cilantro and the pepper for freshness, the soy sauce for saltiness, the pickled ginger that gives the dish a real boost and wake's you up straight away. Then to finish it all off, the soft poached egg or fresh egg gives a creamy and smooth finish.

2½ L (4⅓ pints) chicken stock	3 garlic cloves	pickled or fresh ginger, julienne
250 g (8 oz) jasmine rice	5 cilantro roots, chopped	1 handful cilantro leaves, chopped
200 g (7 oz) soft pork bones	4–5 eggs	fish and soy sauce
400 g (12 oz) pork mince	5 spring onion	black pepper

Bring the stock to the boil and keep more stock¼ on hand because the level of stock will vary.

Pound the rice in a granite mortar to a rough broken consistency. Set aside.

Add the whole garlic and the cilantro roots to the stock. Simmer for 5 minutes then add the raw rice. Cook until the rice is soft. Add the pork bones and cook for 30 minutes adding stock if the porridge is thickening too fast.

While the pork bones are cooking, roll the pork mince into small balls. Add the pork mince balls to the stock. Cook for another 10 minutes until the consistency is to your liking.

Spoon into serving bowls and top with a raw egg or a 2-minute poached egg. Garnish with pickled ginger, cilantro leaves, spring onion and cracked fresh pepper.

Serve the fish sauce and soy sauce as a side.

Thai Food Sensation

RICE CONGEE WITH MINCED PORK

KHAO TOM

SERVES 4–5

This dish is very similar to *Jok*. The difference is that this soup is not cooked as long and the rice is not broken but kept whole. This means the base of the congee is lighter and thinner.

1 L (32 fl oz) chicken stock	1 teaspoon black pepper	garlic, chopped and fried
500 ml (16 fl oz) white rice, cooked	1 handful cilantro leaves	garlic oil (page 27)
500 g (1 lb) pork mince	4–5 poached eggs	fresh chili, chopped
2 tablespoons fish sauce	3–4 spring onions, sliced diagonally	fresh ginger, cut into thin strips

Add stock to a large saucepan. Bring to the boil then add the rice and cook for 30 minutes.

Use both hands to roll the pork mince into small balls. Add to the stock and cook for another 8–10 minutes.

While the pork balls are cooking, boil some water and pour the water into a bowl large enough to hold the eggs. Place the eggs (in their shells) into the boiled water for 3 minutes.

Once the eggs are ready, take out of the water and crack each into separate bowls or cups.

To serve, ladle the congee into the bowls. Garnish with cilantro, black pepper, spring onions, fried garlic, fresh ginger and the egg.

Serve with fish sauce as a side.

Thai Food Sensation

DEEP-FRIED CHINESE BREAD

PAA TONG GOY

MAKES 50 PIECES

This deep-fried bread is one of the most addictive breakfasts you can have. Served plain or with pandanus custard—amazing either way. This bread was introduced by the Chinese and is mostly made by Chinese vendors. It is so popular, it is not uncommon to find a crowd waiting to receive their freshly fried bread. This is best eaten fresh while it's crispy and hot.

2 teaspoons salt	1 kg (35 oz) all-purpose (plain) flour	pandan custard (optional)
3 tablespoons sugar	3 tablespoons oil	cinnamon sugar (optional)
2 teaspoons baking soda (bicarbonate of soda)	vegetable oil	
	500 ml (16 fl oz) water	

Heat oil in a frypan.

In a bowl, mix the salt, sugar and baking soda together. Then add the water and oil and mix well.

In a new mixing bowl, sift the flour, make a well in the center and slowly begin adding about a quarter of the liquid mixture. Kneed the dough until you have a dry crumble.

Slowly add more of the mixture. Kneed the dough. Add more mixture and kneed the dough again.

When all the mixture has been added and you have kneeded the dough, pick up the dough and slam it into the bench—this helps to stretch out the gluten strains. Continue to slam the dough onto the bench until the dough is silky smooth and soft. The dough needs to be quite wet so please do not think its wrong and add more flour.

Place the dough into a new clean bowl and wrap with cling wrap. Allow the dough to rise. When the dough has doubled in size, place the dough on to a clean beach. Take a small potion of the dough at a time and make a long strip, around 15 cm (6 inches) long. Use plenty of flour during this process as the dough will stick to the bench.

Turn the long strip horizontally and cut into 2 cm (¾ inch) strips. Set aside covering them with a wet cloth so the dough does not dry out.

Using one hand, pick up one piece of dough. Use a brush dipped in water to wet the top of the dough then using your free hand, pick up another piece of dough and place it on top of the dampened strip. Using your thumbs, gentle squeeze the dough together—only in the middle of the dough. Set aside to rest for 10 minutes. Repeat with the remaining dough.

Heat the oil in a deep fryer or wok to 180°C (350°F). Deep-fry six at a time until golden. Place onto a paper towel to drain.

Serve the bread with Pandan Custard (page 28) or cinnamon sugar

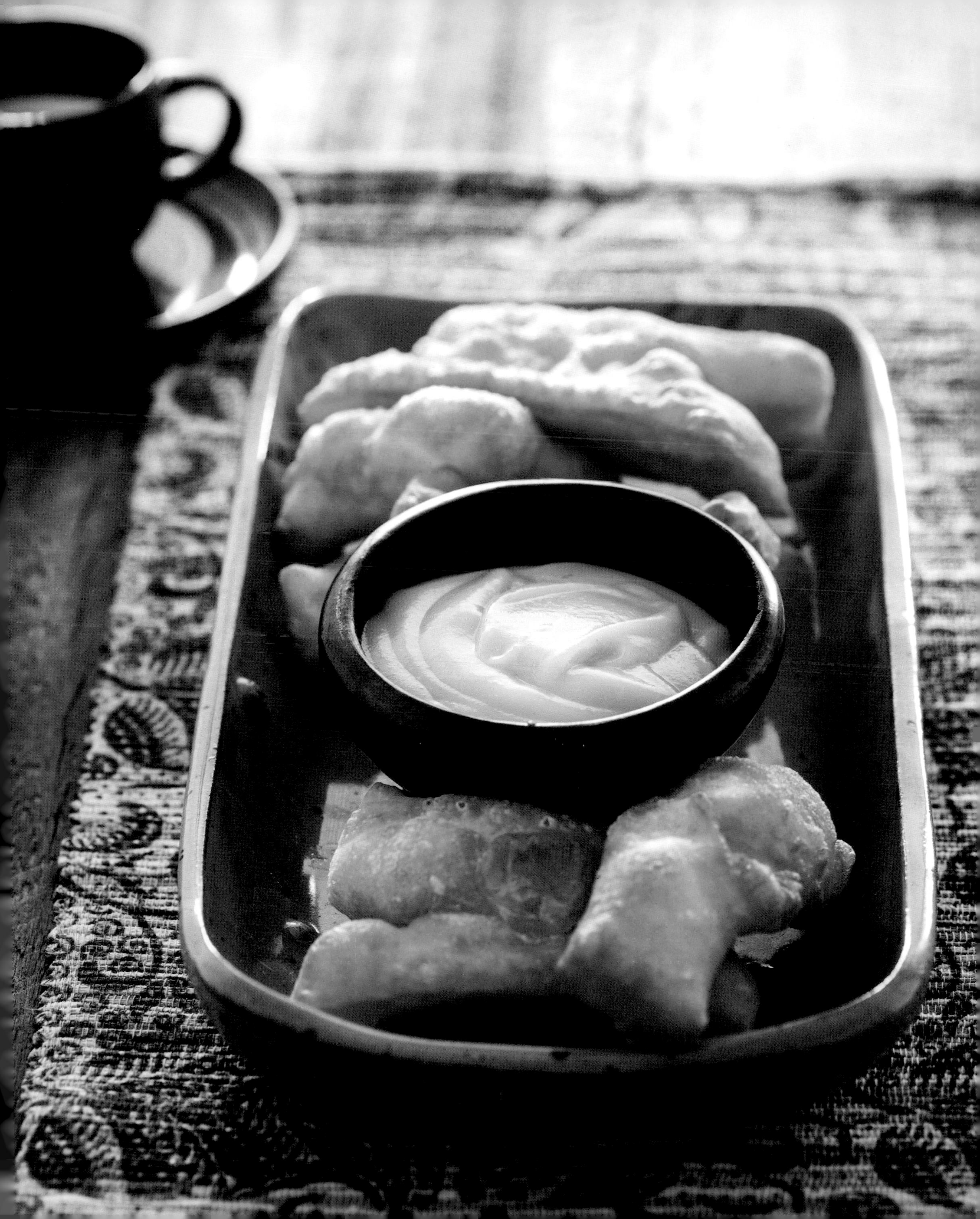

OMELET STUFFED WITH SPICY MINCE PORK

KAI JIEOW MUU

SERVES 4

Kair Jieow Muu is a wonderful breakfast omelet. The pork mince is rich and spicy and the egg binds everything together.

Omelet
8 free range eggs
1 teaspoon fish sauce
2 tablespoons cilantro roots

Stuffing
1 tablespoon rice oil
1 teaspoon garlic
4 Thai chilies
300 g (10 oz) pork mince
2 tablespoons oyster sauce
1 teaspoon sugar
1 handful cilantro leaves

Garnish
handful sawtooth coriander
3 long red chilies, sliced lengthwise

In a saucepan heat the rice oil. Add the garlic and chili and sweat off.

Add the pork and cook until light gray in color then add the oyster sauce and sugar. Simmer until the liquids have been evaporated.

Beat the eggs in a bowl with the fish sauce and the cilantro roots.

In a wok (or omelet pan), add a little oil and when hot, pour the egg mixture into the pan. Pull the egg mixture back to the center of the wok. Lift the wok on a slight angle so the egg mixture runs back to the edge where you started. Do this a few times so the egg mixture cooks evenly and also increases in size.

Once the egg mixture has set on the bottom, add the pork mixture to the center of the omelet. Carefully fold the omelet in half. Place on a plate or long platter. Top with the sawtooth coriander and the long red chilies.

Serve immediately.

STEAMED EGG WITH RED ONION AND FRIED GARLIC

KAI TOON

SERVES 2

1 tablespoon rice oil	6 eggs	6 cilantro roots
2 tablespoons garlic, finely sliced	1½ tablespoons fish sauce	½ handful of cilantro leaves
½ red onion, finely sliced	½ teaspoon white pepper	
175 ml (6 fl oz) water	2 tablespoons spring onions	

In a saucepan, add the oil and bring to a light heat. Add the garlic and red onion and cook to a light golden color. Strain and set aside.

Fill a Thai steamer pot with water and bring to a high steam.

In a heatproof bowl, add the eggs and all of the other ingredients together. Beat the eggs mixture for 2 minutes to combined ingredients. Slowly lower the bowl into the steam basket and cover with a lid.

Steam for 10–15 minutes or until the eggs have risen and are puffy and set. When cooked, be careful you don't burn yourself when removing the bowl.

Serve the eggs immediately in the same bowl as the eggs will lose their fluffiness quite quickly. Serve with rice.

STICKY RICE AND SESAME SEED BEEF

NGAAN NEUA KAAO NIEOW

SERVES 4

This little snack is a wonderful way to have a bite to eat in the morning if you're not overly hungry. The sweetness of the beef with the rich flavor of the sesame seeds is a taste sensation.

- 500 g (1 lb) sticky rice, soaked overnight
- 2 tablespoons oyster sauce
- 2 tablespoons soy sauce
- 2 tablespoons sweet soy
- 1 teaspoon fish sauce
- 4 tablespoons palm sugar
- 800 g (1¾ lb) beef skirt steak
- ½ teaspoon ground white pepper
- 5 tablespoons sesame seeds
- banana leaf
- rice oil

Steam the sticky rice in a Thai bamboo steamer for 30 minutes or until cooked.

In a saucepan, add the oyster sauce, both soy sauces, fish sauce and palm sugar. Bring to a light thickness then set aside.

Slice the beef very finely. Add to the saucepan and cover with the sauce. Add the white pepper and allow the beef to marinate for 20 minutes.

Heat the oil in a frypan to 160°C (320°F). Add the sliced beef, and cook until golden and well colored.

While the beef is cooking, slowly dry cook the sesame seeds in another pan to give the seeds some color.

When the beef is cooked (it will be dark in color), add the sesame seeds.

Place the steamed sticky rice in the middle of the banana leaf, and then top with the sesame beef. Wrap and serve.

CILANTRO AND GARLIC OMELET

PAK CHEE GRA TIAM KAI JIEOW

SERVES 4

Thai omelets are not like French omelets. The middle is normally cooked right through in Thai omelets, whereas in French omelets, the middle is still slightly undercooked to give a creamy feel. The Thai's like their omelets golden in color and cooked.

10 free range eggs
3 tablespoons cilantro roots, diced
1 teaspoon fish sauce

1 tablespoon rice oil
3 teaspoons garlic, diced
handful of cilantro leaves

½ handful bean sprouts
2 tablespoons fried garlic
½ handful Chinese chives

First crack the eggs into a bowl. Add cilantro roots and fish sauce and beat all together.

Heat the rice oil in a frypan and add the garlic. Cook until golden, then add the egg mix and slowly start to move the egg mixture. Start from the outside edge, pull the egg mixture back to the center of the pan. Lift the pan on a slight angle so the egg mixture runs back to the edge where you started. Do this a few times so the egg mixture cooks evenly.

Once the egg is starting to cook, add in the cilantro leaves. When the omelet is almost cooked, (the bottom will be golden), flip the omelet over so that it is golden on both sides.

Serve with rice.

Thai Food Sensation

ROTI WITH CONDENSED MILK AND SUGAR

ROTI NOM KON WAAN

MAKES 6

roti (page 29)
1 tin condensed milk
white sugar
butter

Cut the roti into bite size squares and place on a plate or bowl.

Pour the condensed milk over the top and sprinkle with sugar.

Serve immediately with a strong black coffee.

STICKY RICE CAKE

KAOW GRIAP

SERVES 4

This is an all day snack that is very interesting, if you don't like fish sauce you can take it out and use plain salt or other seasonings. This is a great way to use up any leftover sticky rice—in Thailand no one wastes food.

- 500 g (1 lb) cooked sticky rice
- 3 whole eggs
- 1 tablespoon fish sauce (optional)

Shape the cooked sticky rice into 40–50 g (1½–2 oz) balls. Flatten the balls out to a patty shape.

Beat the eggs and add the fish sauce. Coat the rice patties with the egg mixture. Place on a tray and grill until golden brown.

While grilling the rice cakes, brush with extra egg mixture from time to time to give a more stronger taste.

Once golden brown, take out and serve immediately.

Street Food
and
Snacks

The following recipes are generally served in Thailand in the afternoon—the hottest part of the day. With the morning vendors selling out of food and heading home with their day's earnings, there is little food to find in the early hours of the afternoon, Mind you, the afternoons in Thailand start at 11 am with food vendors coming out from their homes to set up for the afternoon trade that will continue late into the night and into the early hours of the morning. Really, the streets never close—it's 24 hours a day.

The vendors set up their individual street stalls—each one having a different talent that has been past down from generation to generation.

The afternoons are very exciting as there are more food choices. Coals are lit and the Thai grills are ready to serve *Gai Yang*, *Moo Bping*, *Kor Moo Yang* and *Sai Ooua Lanna*—served with sticky rice and a spicy *Nahm Jim*.

The *Pok Pok* noise can be heard as an older lady pounds her terracotta mortar with her wooden pestle making *Som Dtum* salad. There are eggs being smoked and beef boat noodle soup being served. And around every corner, there are many other food stalls selling delicious Thai street food.

The streets are now becoming once again a crazy fun environment to be in. The bustling workers are coming out for a quick break from work, looking for a snack that can be consumed quickly, mostly eaten on the back of a motorbike or that of the market food courts. After 3 pm, the school kids are out of school and vendors are cooking treats and sweets for the kids to consume on their way home.

The footpath is now impossible to walk on so the street is the best way to pass the hungry line of children.

The traffic, like the mornings, is very busy with the afternoon being just that little bit crazier due to everyone finishing work and school. Like the mornings the buses and the taxis are overcrowed with people, all finding any place to sit or stand with bags filled with food and fresh vegetables. The police are directing traffic, although it seems every one does what they want to do.

By mid afternoon, the day is cooling down. People have headed home and the markets are starting to pack down, the street vendors have moved slowly outwards from the market grounds and are now heading directly onto the streets.

FAST FOOD

CRISPY RICE CRACKERS WITH PALM SUGAR

KAOW TAEN

MAKES 15–20

These rice crackers are a wonderful treat and are not too difficult to make, although they do take some time to prepare.

    1 kg (2.2 lb) cooked sticky rice (page 31)
    500 ml (16 fl oz) rice oil
    palm sugar caramel (page 28)

Spread the rice on a tray. If the rice is sticking to your hands, wet your hands with water so that the rice is easier to handle.

Make small flat patties of rice by rolling small amounts into balls. Each ball needs to be flattened to make a disk about 8 cm (3 inch) in diameter and 2–3 mm (1/8 inch) thick—it's important that the crackers and thin so make them as thin as possible.

When you have made the crackers, leave them to sit at room temperature for 7–8 hours (In Thailand, they put them outside in the sun for the duration). Turn them over a few times to make sure they are drying out properly.

When the crackers are dried, heat oil in a frypan to a medium heat. Put 3 crackers into the oil each time. Cook until the rice has puffed up. Turn and cook until the other side has puffed up and both sides are golden in color.

Remove from oil and place on a wire rack or paper towel to cool. Repeat until all crackers are cooked.

Sprinkle with palm sugar caramel and serve.

Thai Food Sensation

FERMENTED PORK SAUSAGES

SAI GROP ISARN

SERVE 3–4

Sai Grop Isan is my all-time favorite street snack. This wonderful fermented pork sausage that is normally served in a small plastic bag and then covered with a spicy *Nahm Jim Gai* (sweet chili sauce) and served with fresh herbs and vegetables and *Kaao Niao* (sticky rice). When making this, it is important to give the pork time to marinate for 2 days. Before you start cooking, check that the aromas are a rich combination of garlic, white pepper and a light sour smell but still really fresh.

Sausage casing
650 g (22 oz) pork belly, skin
    removed and minced
250 g (8 oz) garlic, finely chopped
160 g (5½ oz) cooked jasmine rice
60 g (2 oz) pork fat (from under the
    skin of pork belly)

1 tablespoon salt
2 teaspoons white pepper
1 tablespoon fish sauce

Sides
fresh chilies
fresh ginger

fresh garlic
cabbage
sweet chili sauce (page 42)
sticky rice (page 31)

To make the sausage casing: Clean the casings by adding a handful of salt, vinegar and water in a bowl. Scrub the casings, then rinse very well. (If any holes are made or seen in the process of cleaning, throw out the casing and start again.) Ask your butcher to mince the pork belly for you (make sure the mince has a high fat content).

To make the filling: In a bowl, mix together the pork mince, garlic, rice, fat, salt, pepper and fish sauce. Make sure all ingredients are combined well. Cover the mix and let marinate for 30 minutes. Take the washed casing and, if using a mixer sausage stuffing attachment, place the casing over the nozzle and slowly fill the casing with the pork mince. Alternatively, use a piping bag. Tie off the end with string.

With your hands, add the mixture gently to the casing moving the mince all the way to the bottom of the casing. Fill the casings and then make 3 cm (1½ inch) sausages. Using your fingers, pinch a small amount of the filling at intervals, then twist the sausage to 'tie off' the casing at intervals. Tie off with cooking string to define each sausage.

Allow the string of sausages to rest for 30 minutes before hanging them in a warm area of the house. Allow the sausages to ferment for 1 or 2 days depending on the heat. You can leave them in the refrigerator for 2 days as an alternative.

To cook sausages: Heat the coal grill, once the coals have changed from a bright red to a gray color, place the sausages onto the grill. Make sure you watch the sausages carefully, turning them for even cooking. Once the sausage is firm to the touch, approximately 12–15 minutes, move to the side of the grill and allow to rest for 10 minutes.

Serve whole or sliced on a platter with the sides.

FISH CAKES

TOD MON BPLAA

MAKES ABOUT 15

Thai fish cakes are known to be the most popular starter.

You can use mackerel instead of snapper fillet if you want a more oily fish cake.

350 g (11½ fl oz) red curry paste (page 60)
pickled cucumber (page 29)
700 g (1½ lb) snapper fillet, diced
200 g (7 oz) shrimp (prawn) tails, peeled and deveined
3 tablespoons grachai, diced (from Asian supermarkets)
3 tablespoons pickled ginger, diced

18 kaffir lime leaves, finely sliced
200 g (7 oz) snake beans, very finely sliced
3 pinches of dried chilies flakes
2 eggs
3 cilantro roots, finely sliced
1 lime, zest only
1 tablespoon palm sugar, grated using micro plane

2 tablespoons fish sauce
pinch of salt
500 ml (16 fl oz) rice oil
handful of chilies, sliced
cucumber, diced
lettuce, shredded
cabbage, shredded

Make the red curry paste (page 56) and pickled cucumber (page 29) as per instructions.

Place the fish and shrimp into a food processor and blend to a smooth paste. If the mixture is sticking, use water to loosen. Add water slowly as the mixture should remain firm.

Add the grachai, pickled ginger, kaffir lime leaves and the eggs. Combined all very quickly in the blender. Transfer the mixture into a bowl and add the red curry paste.

Add the cilantro roots, lime zest, snake beans, chili flakes, palm sugar and fish sauce. Taste the mixture to check the seasoning. Add salt if desired. (I like to taste it raw as that gives me a true indication of what is needed or what needs to be adjusted)

Wet your hands, take a small amount of the mixture and roll it into a ball and then flatten to make fish cakes about 5–6 cm (2–2.5 inches) round and about 1½ cm (½ inch) thick. Place on a tray and continue to make the fish cakes until you use all the mixture.

Heat the oil in a deep saucepan or deep fryer.

When the oil is ready, place a few in at a time—not too many as the oil will cool and be adsorbed into the cakes. Turn a few times and cook until dark golden brown. Drain on a paper towel.

Serve with pickled cucumber, fresh chilies, cucumber, lettuce and cabbage.

by adding the crushed peanuts, herbs and the diced cucumber. Add the peanuts to the pickled cucumber just before serving.

Thai Food Sensation

CHICKEN SATAY

SATAY GAI

SERVES 4

600 g (1⅓ lb) chicken thighs, halved
    lengthways

The marinade
1½ tablespoons cilantro seeds
1 teaspoon cumin seeds
1½ teaspoons turmeric powder (or
    3 teaspoons fresh turmeric)
4 tablespoons lemongrass, chopped

pinch of salt
1 tablespoon galangal
125 ml (4 fl oz) coconut cream
2 tablespoons palm sugar
2 tablespoons rice oil

The sauce
3 tablespoons palm sugar

125 g (4 oz) roasted nuts, semi
    crushed (page 29)
2 tablespoons fish sauce
1 teaspoon chili powder
125 ml (4 fl oz) coconut milk
1 tablespoon oil

Side
pickled cucumber (page 29)

In a cast iron pan, dry roast the cilantro and cumin seeds until aromatic. In a granite mortar, grind the spices to a fine powder then add the turmeric powder. Mix well. In a large mortar, add the lemongrass, galangal and salt and pound to a fine paste. Add the combined dry spices powder and mix well.

Mix together the coconut cream, sugar and salt in a bowl until sugar and salt have dissolved.

Add the paste to the coconut liquid then add the chicken tenderloins. Make sure the chicken is well mixed into the paste. Cover with cling wrap and allow to marinate in the refrigerator overnight. Soak the bamboo skewers overnight. Thread the chicken pieces on to the bamboo skewers.

If using a coals grill, heat until red hot and then allow the coals to become gray before cooking. If using an oven grill or barbecue, set on a medium heat and cook for 10 minutes or until cooked.

To make the satay paste, in a medium saucepan add a small amount of oil, add the paste and allow to simmer for 10 minutes until fragrant then add the coconut cream.

Simmer for 10 minutes add the coconut milk, palm sugar and the peanuts. Simmer until the satay sauce is thick. Finish the satay sauce with the fish sauce and the chilly powder. Take off the heat and allow to cool for 1 hour.

Serve with satay sauce and cucumber.

GRILLED PORK SKEWERS

MOO BPING

SERVES 4

These pork skewers can be found all over Thailand. This popular Isarn snack goes well with sticky rice.

1.5 kg (3⅓ lb) pork neck
300 g (10 oz) pork back fat
Marinade
4 tablespoons dark soy sauce

2 tablespoons oyster sauce
4 tablespoons fish sauce
6 tablespoons vegetable oil
6 cilantro roots

4 teaspoons garlic, sliced
4 tablespoons palm sugar
½ teaspoon pepper

Soak bamboo skewers overnight in water.

In a bowl combine they soy, oyster and fish sauces with the vegetable oil to make the marinade. Slice the garlic and cilantro roots and add these to the bowl.

Slice the pork neck and fat into thin strips. Add the pork to the marinade and allow to sit for a minimum of 2 hours, preferably overnight. Keep the pork fat in the refrigerator until needed.

Heat the coals until they are red hot and allow them to turn gray; or heat barbecue grill or oven grill to moderate heat.

Thread the pork neck on the skewers making sure to fold the pork neck a few times. Place the pork back fat onto the end of each skewer—this will allow the pork to stay moist.

Grill for 25–30 minutes. Serve with sticky rice and a plate of fresh vegetables.

STUFFED CHICKEN WINGS

PPIIK GAI YAT SAI

SERVES 4–5

I haven't met anyone who doesn't like this recipe. The time to debone the chicken wings is worth the effort. These are an amazing starter and are a lot of fun to make.

20 chicken wings, de-boned

Paste
5 birds-eye chilies
1 teaspoon of salt
3 lemongrass, sliced very fine (purple part only)
13 cloves of garlic, pound
6 slices galangal
3 tablespoon cilantro root, sliced

6 kaffir lime leaf, sliced finely
1½ teaspoon coriander seed
1½ teaspoon white pepper powder
2 tablespoon pickled ginger
pinch of Gapi (shrimp paste)

Stuffing
600 g (1⅓ lb) pork mince
200 g (7 oz) prawns, diced
200 g (7 oz) vermicelli noodles

1 handful cilantro leaves, sliced
1 handful spring onions, sliced
6 tablespoons fish sauce
3 tablespoons thin soy sauce
1 tablespoon kecap manis (Indonesian sweet soy sauce)
5 tablespoons coconut cream
1 egg
rice oil for frying

Make the paste as per instructions on page 56.

For the stuffing, soak the vermicelli noodles in cold water for 40 minutes. Remove and cut the noodles with scissors into 1 cm (1/8 inch) lengths.

In a large bowl, add the paste with the stuffing ingredients. Mix until all ingredients are combined well. Stuff the chicken wings with the mixture, making sure the chicken wings are full.

Bring a bamboo steamer to a rapid heat. Line the bottom of the steamer with baking paper. Add about 5 chicken wings at a time and steam for 8 minutes. Take out and pat dry with absorbent paper. Repeat until all the wings are steamed.

In a large wok or deep fryer, fry the chicken wings until they are golden and crispy.

Serve with fresh herbs such as Vietnamese mint and an arrangement of dipping sauces. They go well with sweet chili sauce (page 42).

TURMERIC GRILLED CHICKEN

GAI YAANG KAMIN

SERVES 4

Gai Yaang Kamin can be seen grilling all over Thailand. Consumed daily, there are many different ingredients and marinades that can be used. The most common stuffing is with lemongrass. A coal grill is the best choice for this dish to have the true Thai flavor experience.

1 free range chicken, approximately
    1½ kg (3⅓ lb)
1 tablespoon thin soy sauce
1 tablespoon fish sauce

Paste
1 tablespoon fresh turmeric
3 cilantro roots, chopped
8 cloves garlic, chopped

1 teaspoon white pepper
1 tablespoon white sugar
1 teaspoon salt

To make the paste, pound all the ingredients together.

Cut the chicken in half and remove the tail back bone. Place the halved chicken in a large bowl. Add the paste, soy sauce, salt and fish sauce. Mix well and marinate for 2 hours or overnight if time allows. Heat the coals to a bright red then allow the coals to turn gray. Grill the chicken for 15 minutes each side depending on how large the chicken is. Keep an eye on the chicken as the coals are very hot. If the skin burns a little, do not worry as it gives a smoky flavor. However, avoid excessive burning.

Chop the chicken into pieces and serve with a selection of sides such as green papaya salad (page 115), sweet chili sauce (page 42), sweet tamarind sauce (page 41) and sticky rice (page 31).

SON-IN-LAW EGGS

KAI LEUK KOEY

SERVES 5

A funny name for a dish but this is the favorite that just about every Thai mother has made for her kids—basically fried boiled eggs.

10–15 eggs, fresh and room
    temperature
rice oil for deep-frying
banana leaf, cut into the size of the
    plate (optional)

The Sauce
125 ml (4 fl oz) water
125 g (4 oz) palm sugar
6 long red chilies, de-seeded and
    diced
8 cilantro roots, washed
1 small red onion, diced
4 garlic cloves, sliced
4 tablespoons fish sauce
2 whole limes, juiced
4 tablespoons tamarind water
    (page 41)

Garnish
fried red long chilies (page 26)
fried shallots (page 27)
fried garlic (page 27)
1 long red chili, finely julienned
fresh Thai basil leaves
fresh cilantro leaves

To make the sauce, in a saucepan, add the water, tamarind water and palm sugar and bring to a syrup-like consistency. Add the red onion, chilies, cilantro root and cook for 10 minutes. Take off the heat and allow to cool for 15 minutes. Once cool, add the cilantro leaves, lime juice and fish sauce. Taste and adjust if needed. The dressing should have a balance of sweet, sour and spicy.

In a large pot, fill with water and bring to a rapid boil. Slowly add the eggs to the water and cook for 6 minutes. While the eggs are cooking, prepare an ice bucket by adding ice to a large container of water so the water is freezing cold. Once eggs are cooked, quickly transfer the eggs into the iced water and allow to cool completely. Peel the eggs and set aside.

Heat the oil in a wok or deep fryer to 180°C (350°F). Slowly add the eggs one by one making sure they are submerged. Cook until the eggs are golden brown, about 3 minutes. Take out and drain eggs on paper towels.

Place the banana leaf on a serving plate or bowl. With a knife stab the eggs and then slightly squeeze the egg to break the yolk and cover with the sauce. Top the eggs with a selection of garnishes.

Serve with a selection of sides such as cucumber, lettuce and jasmine rice (page 30).

Thai Food Sensation

SALTY DRIED BEEF

NEUA KEM/NEUA DAET DIOW

SERVES 3

A wonderful snack that tastes amazing. In Thailand, the beef is air dried in the sun for up to 38 hours. For this recipe, I suggest you keep the meat outside for at least half a day, or keep in the fridge uncovered for the same amount of time, as this will dry the meat out.

500 g (16 oz) beef rump or chuck
    steak
4 tablespoons soy sauce

10 tablespoons oyster sauce
2–3 tablespoons sugar
½ teaspoon white pepper

2 garlic cloves
rice oil for deep frying

Slice the beef into thin slices. Combined with all the other ingredients and allow to marinate of 2 hours. Place the meat onto a tray covered with a fly net. Allow the meat to sit in the sun or keep in the refrigerator uncovered for up to 8 hours.

Heat the oil to 180°C (350°F). Add in the dried beef and cook for 10 minutes or until golden. Make sure the beef is golden on each side.

Serve with a selection of sides including Thai chilies, cos lettuce, roast tomato relish (see page 36) or sticky rice (see page 31).

GRILLED BANANA WITH COCONUT SUGAR CARAMEL

GLUAY BPING NAHM DTAAN CHUUAM

MAKES 10

Kluay is Thai for banana. *Kluay Nahm Wa* is a variety of banana that is sticky and sweet when ripe. They hold their shape more than the bananas found in supermarkets, which should not be used as they lose their shape. Look for *Kluay Nahm Wa* hanging above the cashier in many Asian supermarkets. They are more expensive than regular bananas, but worth it. In Thailand *Gluay Bping Nahm Dtaan Saai* is normally served in a plastic pocket, the caramel is poured over the top of the bananas and then served.

10 kluay nahm wa banana, peeled

Caramel
375 g (12 oz) coconut sugar
125 ml (4 fl oz) coconut cream

58 g (2 oz) butter, room temperature
10 bamboo skewers, soaked in water
   for 30 minutes

To make the caramel, heat a pan and add the sugar over a low heat. Bring it to a smooth consistency then add in the coconut cream. Simmer until the liquid reduces to a thick syrup. Cool to room temperature and add the butter. Add a pinch of salt if you like a salted caramel. Stir to combine.

Light the coals and heat until red hot then allow the coals to turn gray in color. If not using a coal grill, an oven grill will work fine.

Skewer the bananas then grill for 10–15 minutes. The flesh should be soft but still firm and not falling apart.

Arrange bananas in a bowl or on a plate. Pour caramel over and serve.

GRILLED PORK NECK

KOR MUU YAANG

SERVES 4

Kor Muu Yaang is by far the best way to cook pork on the planet. The marinade doesn't taste that good by itself but something amazing happens while the meat is grilling. The condensed milk caramelizes, the white pepper and salt flavors come out to create the most mouth-watering pork heaven in the world. The condensed milk also helps to soften the pork neck allowing the salt, pepper, garlic and soy sauce flavors to fuse with the pork.

800 g (1¾ lb) pork neck or belly, cut into 4 potions

Marinade
395 g (13 oz) condensed milk
2 tablespoons palm sugar
½ teaspoon pepper

2 garlic cloves, sliced
3 tablespoon thin soy sauce
2 tablespoons salt

Sides
fresh Thai chilies
cabbage

cucumber
bunch of fresh herbs
sticky rice (page 31)
sweet chili sauce (page 43) or tamarind caramel (page 39)

To make the marinade, add all the ingredients to a bowl and set aside until needed.

Wash the pork neck well then pat dry. Add the pork neck to the marinade and leave overnight or even better, for 48 hours in the refrigerator.

Light the coals and wait until the coals are gray in color. Grill for 45 minutes or until the pork is cooked through. Thai people like their pork completely cook, however cook it to your liking.

When cooked, remove from heat and allow to rest for around 10 minutes.

Slice and serve with a selection of sides including fresh Thai chilies, cabbage, sticky rice or chili sauce.

FRIED OYSTER BEEF

HOI NAANG ROM NEUA

SERVES 4

Fried oyster beef is very similar to dried beef, although this is the non-fermented oyster sauce style. The beef can be fried or grilled, depending on what you like. Use any cut of beef with a high fat content.

500 g (16 oz) chuck steak
125 ml (4 fl oz) oyster sauce
2 tablespoons sugar
1 cilantro root

1 tablespoon fish sauce
pinch of salt
vegetable oil

Slice the meat into thin slices and put into a large bowl. Add the oyster sauce, cilantro root, fish sauce and the sugar. Marinate for 6 hours or overnight.

In a wok heat the oil to 180°C (350°F) then add the meat. Cook for approximately 10 to 15 minutes or until the beef is nicely caramelized. Transfer to a paper towel to drain.

Serve with a selection of sides including snake beans, roast banana pepper relish (page 37) or sticky rice (see page 31).

THAI SALADS

CRYING TIGER

SEUA RONG HAI

SERVES 2–4

Anyone who loves Thai food may have had this spicy Thai beef salad once or twice. It is very spicy with bursts of freshness from the lime and tamarind. It's extremely addictive and very healthy, with no oil.

Make sure you use the very best cut of meat. It's very important to rest the meat after grilling for the same length of time as for cooking. This will allow the meat to relax and the marinade flavors to filter through the meat to keep it moist and tender.

300 g (10 oz) beef tender loin or
    scotch fillet

The marinade
90 ml (2 fl oz) of soy sauce
90 ml (2 fl oz) black sweet soy sauce
90 ml (2 fl oz) oyster sauce
pinch of pepper
2 tablespoons white sugar
3 garlic cloves, sliced
2 cilantro roots
1 tablespoon fish sauce

The dressing
3 dried long red chilies, fried and
    crushed
4 Thai chili, sliced
3 Thai shallots, sliced
2 garlic cloves
4 tablespoons tamarind pulp
3 tablespoons fish sauce
1 lime, juiced
2 cilantro roots
1 tablespoon palm sugar

6 cherry tomatoes, sliced in halve
3 tablespoons ground rice powder
    (page 28)

Sides
lettuce
cucumber
limes
sticky rice (page 31) or jasmine rice
    (page 30)

Combine all the marinade ingredients together in a bowl. Add the meat to the marinade and leave for 4 hours, or overnight if time allows.

Once the meat has marinated, light the coals so that they become red-hot and then turn gray. Place meat onto the grill and cook for 10–12 minute each side depending on the thickness of the meat. Cook to medium to remain very tender.

While the tenderloin is grilling, put the palm sugar and garlic into the mortar and pound to a paste. Add the cilantro root, sliced shallots and chilies. Bruise a little to allow the oils to be released. Add the fish sauce, lime juice and tamarind pulp and mix well. Add the cherry tomato but don't pound.

Take the meat off the grill and allow to rest for the same amount of cooking time. Slice the meat into thin bite size slices no more than 6 mm (¼ inch thick against the grain). The dressing can be added to the beef and then plated, or served on the side. Just before serving, add the sticky rice powder to the dressing.

KING SHRIMP SALAD

YUM GONG

SERVE 4

1 kg (2.2 lb) fresh king prawns

The dressing
3 tablespoons thom yum paste (page 31)
2 tablespoons palm sugar
4 tablespoons fish sauce
4 tablespoon lime juice

The salad
3 tablespoons pickled ginger, washed and drained

1 lemongrass stalk, purple part sliced finely
1 handful pointed cilantro (sawtooth coriander), torn
1 handful cilantro, torn
3 spring onions, sliced
1 large red onion, finely sliced
4 long red chilies, sliced on an angle
4 kaffir lime leaves, sliced julienne very finely

½ handful coconut flesh, shaved and roasted
1 handful Chinese chives, cut into 2 cm (¾ inch) lengths
1 handful bean sprouts, washed and drained
1 handful dried shrimp floss, (page 30)
1 banana leaf, for plating (optional)

This salad will impress your guests with a burst of flavors that are sure to delight. The shrimp can be grilled or blanched in salted boiling water. Grilling will give them a smoky rich flavor, the blanched shrimp will take on more of the flavor of the dressing. Both ways are great although I love grilled shrimp.

When buying shrimp, fresh is by far the best. However, frozen will suffice. Make sure you defrost them in the refrigerator overnight on a drip tray. Please do not defrost in water, as the shrimp will be water logged.

To make the dressing, heat the palm sugar in a saucepan until it dissolves. Add the thom yum paste and slowly sweat off the paste, allowing the paste to become slightly golden. Add the fish sauce and lime juice. Set aside and allow the dressing to cool completely.

Peel the inner body shell off the shrimp and keep for later use (for a stock or a soup). Keep the heads and tail on the shrimp. Using a knife very slowly slice the back of the shrimp to reveal the intestine. Pull out and discard. Wash the shrimp under water to remove any grit.

Either grill or blanch the shrimp. If grilling on a coal grill, heat the coals to red, then allow the coals to became gray before cooking. Oil the grill before placing the shrimp on. Barbecue or over grill will suffice. Cook shrimp for 4 to 5 minutes (depending on the size) turning once. Take care when turning to not break the head off the shrimp. If blanching, heat a large pot of salted water. Once boiling, add the shrimp. Simmer for 5 to 6 minutes and then drain. This needs to be done at the very last moment before serving.

To make the salad, add the ginger, lemongrass, cilantro, spring onion, red onion, chilies, kaffir lime, Chinese chives, bean sprouts and roasted coconut into a bowl and mix all together. Add the dressing in small amounts at a time to the salad only to cover the salad. Add the shrimp to the salad and toss all together.

Place the banana leaf on the plate. Place salad on the banana leaf creating height and fullness. Sprinkle with shrimp floss and serve immediately.

Serve with a selection of sides, including jasmine rice (page 30).

SALMON GRILLED IN A BANANA LEAF

AEB

SERVES 4

This pocket of joy called *Aeb* is a must to try at home. All the oils, juices and flavor are captured inside the banana leaf parcel. Traditionally eaten with sticky rice, it can be served on a bed of holy basil or lemon basil.

4 x 190 g (6 oz) salmon fillet, flesh
    sliced in halve
1 packet of banana leaves

The paste
8 dried red chilies, soaked, drained
    and chopped
6 Thai bird's eye chilies, sliced
9 garlic cloves, sliced
2 medium shallots, sliced
2 lemongrass stalks, sliced
1 kaffir lime, zested
1 tablespoon turmeric
1 tablespoon cilantro root

The salad
1 pickled mango, julienne or sour
    green mango (purchased)
2 lemongrass, purple part only, sliced
    finely
1 shallot, finely sliced
3 red long chili, de-seeded, julienne
6 kaffir lime leaves julienne
1 handful Vietnamese mint leaves,
    torn
½ handful western mint, torn
1 large knob fresh ginger, julienne
3 tablespoons dried shrimp, chopped

1 Thai banana, grilled and chopped
1 handful cilantro leaves
1 tablespoon dried shrimp

Salad dressing
2 whole limes
3 tablespoons fish sauce
1 tablespoon palm sugar

Garnish
fried shallots (page 27)
fried garlic (page 27)

To make the paste, pound all ingredients to a semi paste, not too smooth but not too chunky. Pounding for 15 minutes should be plenty.

Add salmon pieces to a large bowl (there should be eight: four with skin on, four without). Add the curry paste and mix well using gloved-covered hands. Wrap the fish as per instructions for cooking with banana leaves (page 184). Place the parcels on the grill and cook for 6 to 8 minutes each side for a totally cooking time of about 16 minutes. Don't worry if the banana leaf burns slightly as it is there to protect the fish.

While the salmon is grilling, make the salad and dressing. Combine all the ingredients for the salad in a bowl. Combine the dressing ingredients and add to the salad. Mix well.

To assemble, open the parcel and place the fish (still in the banana leaf) on plates. Top with salad and your choice of garnish. Serve with jasmine or sticky rice.

SASHIMI OF KINGFISH, PARMELO, CASHEW NUT HERB SALAD

SASIMI

SERVE 2

Every one love fresh sashimi. This recipe with the combination of parmelo, cashew nuts and fresh herbs creates flavors that are sweet, sour and fresh.

300 g (10 oz) fresh kingfish, sliced
very thinly (Sashimi style)

The salad
3 long red chilies, de seeded, julienne
1 shallot, finely sliced

6 kaffir lime leaves, julienne
2 springs onion, finely sliced
½ pomelo or pink grapefruit,
segmented
½ handful cilantro leaves
½ handful pointed cilantro

½ handful Vietnamese mint leaves
1 handful cashew nuts, roasted and
semi crushed
seafood dipping sauce (page 35)

Slice the kingfish sashimi style or ask your fishmonger to do it for you.

Place the slices of kingfish on a flat platter or bowl. Top with most of the Nahm Jim making sure that the kingfish is covered with the dressing. In a bowl, mix the salad together, add the rest of the Nahm Jim to the salad and mix well. Top the kingfish with the salad.

Serve with jasmine rice (page 30).

GREEN PAPAYA SALAD

SOM DTAM THAI

SERVES 4

This salad is a favourite and is the most widely eaten salad in Thailand; always served at the dinner table. This version is popular in Bangkok.

The dressing
2 garlic cloves
4 chilies, fresh
2 tablespoons soft palm sugar
2–3 tablespoons fish sauce
2–3 tablespoons lime juice

The salad
8 cherry tomatoes
650 g (22 oz) green papaya, shredded
½ bunch snake beans, cut to 2.5 cm (1 inch)

1 lime cut into small wedges
3 tablespoons roasted peanuts
2 tablespoons dried shrimp

Heat a cast iron pan to high heat, add the dried shrimp and very quickly give them a light frying. This will refresh their flavor and give an extra crisp.

In the mortar pound the peanuts to a chuncky consistency, set aside.

Using a terracotta mortar and a wooden pestle, pound the garlic and the chilies to a light paste keeping the garlic and chili still quite visible. Add the soft palm sugar, the lime wedges and lightly bruise then add the green snake beans, very gentle bruise the beans.

Add the fish sauce and the lime juice.

Add the papaya and the cherry tomatoes and very lightly bruise all, using a large spoon to help move the papaya around as you pound from the side of the mortar. It is very important to pound from the side and not directly above as this will smash the ingredients and not bruise them.

Add the peanuts and the shrimp.

Serve with jasmine or sticky rice (page 31).

ISARN STYLE PAPAYA SALAD

SOM DTAM LAO

SERVES 4

This *Som Dtam* is the from the Loa/Isarn region and is the oldest form of *Som Dtam*. It is not for the weak of heart: it is very pungent, spicy and at first, extremely strong. The more you try, the more you'll love it.

2 garlic cloves
4 Thai chilies
2 tablespoon soft palm sugar
1 whole salted crab (Thai brand)
1 tablespoon fish sauce

1½ tablespoons fermented fish
    sauce (*Nahm Bplaa Raa*)
½ lime, cut into small wedges
½ lime, juiced
6 cherry tomatoes

452 g (15 oz) shredded papaya
1 tablespoon dried shrimp
½ bunch snake bean, cut to 2.5 cm
    (1 inch)
splash tamarind water (optional)

Heat a cast iron pan to high heat, add the dried shrimp and very quickly give them a light fry. This will refresh their flavor and give an extra crisp

Using a large terracotta mortar and a wooden pestle, pound the garlic and chilies keeping the garlic and chili still quite visible in the paste. Add the palm sugar and mix well. Add the lime wedges and lightly bruise. Then add the green snake beans and the black salted crab and very gentle bruise the beans and crab. (Do not smash the crab to a fine paste; the crab is to add flavor and is not to be eaten)

Add the fish sauce and the lime juice. If using the tamarind water, add to the papaya now.

Add the papaya and the cherry tomatoes to the mortar and very lightly bruise all. Use a large spoon to help move the papaya around as you pound from the side of the mortar. It is very important to pound from the side and not from directly above to prevent smashing and bruising the ingredients.

Serve with jasmine rice (page 30).

THAI CUCUMBER SALAD

TAM TAENG KWAA

SERVES 4

This cucumber salad is from the Isarn region, part of the *Som Dtam* family—a really refreshing salad. My wife and children love them.

- 4 small cucumbers, cut into 4 then angle sliced 2.5 cm (1 inch) thick
- 1 tablespoon fish sauce
- 2 tablespoons lime juice
- 6 cherry tomatoes

- ½ bunch of snake beans, chopped to 2 cm (¾ inch)
- 4 Thai chilies
- 2 tablespoons soft palm sugar
- 2 garlic cloves

- 3 tablespoons crushed roasted peanuts
- 200 g (7 oz) of vermicelli noodles
- 1 tablespoon fermented fish sauce (optional)
- 1 tablespoon chili powder

To cook vermicelli noodles, ¾ fill a saucepan of water and bring to the boil. Add the dry noodles and cook as per package instructions. Once cooked, cool under running water.

In a mortar, pound the garlic and the chili to a rough consistency. Add the palm sugar and snake beans and pound slightly. Add the lime juice, fish sauce, cherry tomatoes and cucumber and lightly pound for about 10 seconds so that the cucumber is slightly bruised. Add the crushed peanuts and mix well with a spoon.

Place the vermicelli noodles on the bottom of the bowl, add the salad and serve immediately.

Serve with a side of jasmine rice (page 30).

MIXED NUT SALAD

YUM TUA

SERVES 2–3

This is a beautiful salad that has two of my favorite nuts. The textures and freshness of this salad comes from the herbs, the pineapple and apple. This salad can be added to any meal. The balance is sweet, sour, spicy and salty.

The dressing
4 tablespoons fish sauce
4 tablespoons lime juice
2 tablespoons palm sugar
1 tablespoon tamarind water

The salad
300 g (10 oz) roasted cashew nuts

300 g (10 oz) of roasted macadamia
    nuts
1 red onion, finely sliced
3 long red chilies, sliced
3 spring onion, sliced
2 kaffir lime leaves, julienne
½ pink lady apple, peeled and diced

3 tablespoons pineapple, diced
1 teaspoon lemongrass, finely sliced
1 tablespoon pickled ginger
1 handful cilantro
1 handful mint, torn

In a saucepan gentle heat the palm sugar until it has melted. Add the tamarind water and cook for 2 minutes on the lowest flame. Take off the heat and cool. Add the lime juice and the fish sauce

Roast the nuts separately in the oven until golden and allow the nuts to cool completely. Lightly pound. In a bowl, add all the salad ingredients together. Add the dressing and mix well.

Serve immediately with a selection of sides such as jasmine rice (page 30), sticky rice (page 31) or any savory dishes.

SPICY MINCED CHICKEN SALAD

LAAP GAI ISAN

SERVES 2–3

Laab (*Laap*) is an intense salad packed full of flavor. Laab is a Northern dish that is completely different to that of Laab Isan. Laab Isan is mostly packed with fresh herbs, chilies and has a wet dressing. Cooked with almost any protein in a stock base that is simmered. The salad is combined warm and flavored with burnt sticky rice powder. Northern Laab named Laab Meuang is highly spiced, enriched with offal and blood, mince by hand with a large meat clever to a fine paste and then fried.

The dressing
2 tablespoons palm sugar
3 tablespoons lime juice
2 tablespoons fish sauce
1 tablespoon thin soy sauce

The salad
300 g (10 oz) chicken breast, minced by hand

50 g (2 oz) each of chicken tripe, heart, liver and kidney – optional, minced by hand
375 ml (13 fl oz) water or chicken stock (page 51)
3 red shallots sliced, thinly
125 g (4 oz) of crispy pork skin
3 Thai chilies sliced finely
½ lime zest julienne very finely
3 kaffir lime leaf julienne very finely

2 spring onion sliced finely
2 lemongrass stalks, purple part only, sliced fine
1 handful of western mint leaves, torn
1 handful of cilantro leaves, torn
½ bunch of sawtooth coriander, torn
3 tablespoon chili flakes (page 26)
2 tablespoon roasted rice powder (page 28)

Add all the dressing ingredients together and set aside.

Place all the ingredients into their own separated bowls, set aside until needed.

In a large wok heat the stock or water. Once simmering, add the chicken mince and the offal if using. Cook for 7 minutes or until the chicken is cooked. Strain most of the left over liquid reserving a small amount. Place all the ingredients together, stir and serve immediately with a side of jasmine rice (page 30), cos lettuce or sticky rice (page 31).

SEARED SCALLOP, GRILLED PORK ON BETEL LEAF WITH LIME AND TAMARIND CARAMEL

MIANG

SERVES 7

Miang is normally served in individual side bowls of each ingredient. Guests choose what they want to place onto their betel leaf before being topped with dark toasted caramel and then rolled and eaten all together.

The pork
250 g (8 oz) pork belly, skin on, de-boned
1 tablespoon fish sauce
1 tablespoon kecap maris
1 ½ tablespoons oyster sauce
½ tablespoons tamarind water
½ teaspoon gapi paste
1 pinch white sugar
1 garlic, sliced
4 steams cilantro, chopped
1 chili, sliced
1 kaffir lime leaf, torn
15 scallops, washed then pat dry with paper towel

The salad
3 limes, finely diced
1 kaffir lime zest, finely diced
6 kaffir lime leaves, julienne
2 Thai shallots, julienne
8 tablespoons fried cashew nuts, finely chopped (see roasted nuts, page 29)
8 tablespoons fried macadamia nuts, finely chopped (see roasted nuts, page 29)
1 long red chili, de-seed, julienne very finely
1 spring onion, julienne very finely

2 tablespoons dried shrimp, chopped fine
½ handful cilantro leaves, picked from stalk
3 tablespoons pickled ginger, diced finely
5 tablespoons sweet pineapple, diced finely
15 betel leaves or spinach leaves

Salad dressing
2 teaspoons chili jam
lime juice
oil for cooking scallops

Marinate the pork with all the ingredient for 3 hours. For best results, leave overnight.

Grill the pork over hot coals until cooked, the pork should have a good amount of caramelization. Allow the pork to rest for 15 minutes before cutting. Remove the skin, discard. Slice the pork, then dice into small piece. Add any remaining juice to the diced pork.

Clean the scallops by removing any coral or white membrane, wash well. Heat the skillet pan or grill. Lightly oil the pan then add the scallops, laying them flat, cook for 4 minutes on each side. Slice the scallop thinly, place into a bowl.

Wash the betel leaves and dry well. Prepare all the ingredients keeping them in all their own bowls until needed. Have the tamarind caramel room temp so that it's easy to incorporate.

Once all the ingredients are ready to be combined, place the betel leaves on the plate being served. Spoon a generous amount of the caramel onto the betel leaf. In a bowl add all the salad ingredients with the diced pork and the scallops and lightly dress with the chili jam. Divide the salad between all of the betel leaves. Serve.

SQUID AND SHRIMP SALAD WITH CHILI AND LIME

YAM PLA MEUK

SERVES 3

Everyone loves a good shrimp salad. This is by far the most fresh, mouth-exploding salad you will eat as it has many different flavors and textures.

2 Thai chilies
3 tablespoon lime juice
1 tablespoon palm sugar
1–2 tablespoon fish sauce
3 pieces of salted black crab

The salad
350 g (12 oz) squid
350 g (12 oz) shrimp (prawns), tail on
2 red shallots, finely sliced
1 lemongrass, finely sliced
2 long red chilies, sliced angularly

1 small cucumber, sliced
½ handful of Western mint leaves, torn
½ handful of Vietnamese mint leaves, torn
1 handful of cilantro leaves, torn

Pound the chilies to a paste, then add the liquids and the black salted crab, mix well. Once all is combined set aside.

Score the squid tubes by running a knife along the flesh very lightly, hold the knife on an angle to make diagonal cuts, then cut the squid tubes into 3 cm (about 1 in) strips and the tentacles into 2 cm (¾ in) lengths. Peel the shrimps, leaving the tails on. Butterfly the shrimps and remove the intestines. Set a side.

Fill a large saucepan with salted water and bring to the boil. While waiting for the water to come to the boil, slice all your red shallots and lemongrass very finely and dice the cucumber. Tear the herbs roughly. Once the water is boiling plunge the seafood in and out of the water for 3 minutes or until cooked.

Place into a bowl, add the dressing and allow to sit for 1 minute. Add the remaining ingredients and place immediately.

Serve immediately with a side of jasmine rice (page 30) or sticky rice (see page 31)

THAI CURRIES AND SOUPS

RED CURRY OF DUCK AND LYCHEE

GAENG DAENG BPET

SERVES 4

The paste
red curry paste, (page 60)
Add these ingredients to basic recipe:
½ nutmeg, roasted and pounded
3 cloves, roasted and pounded

The duck
1 duck breast
5 duck legs
handful of salt
duck fat or oil to cover

The curry
125 g (4 oz) red curry paste
250 ml (8 fl oz) coconut cream
500 ml (16 fl oz) coconut milk
500 ml (16 fl oz) chicken stock
   (page 51)
2–3 tablespoons palm sugar
3 tablespoons fish sauce
6 kaffir lime leaves, torn
4 long red chilies, sliced lengthways
½ handful Thai scuds, whole
1 handful Thai basil
300 g (10 oz) fresh lychee (for
   tinned lychee, wash three times)

Garnish
Thai basil
red chili, julienne
kaffir lime leaves, julienne

Pre-heat the oven to 180°C (350°F). Rub the duck legs with a handful of salt and allow to cure for 1 hour. Cover the bottom of a baking tray with baking paper. Wash the duck legs. Pat dry and sit the legs on top of the baking paper. Cover with duck fat or oil until the legs are completely covered. Heat the tray over a gas top until the oil starts to simmer the duck leg. Place into the oven, cook for 2 hour or until duck is just falling off the bone. Heat a cast iron pan with a little duck fat or oil, Place the breast skin side down. Cook for 6 minutes or until the skin is golden then turn the breast. Place into the over for 17 minutes, turn the breast now and then. Allow the duck breast to rest before slicing into 4 cm (1½ inch) slices.

Set aside to cool, once cooled take one leg and remove all the meat from the bone.

In a large saucepan add the coconut milk and chicken stock and bring to a simmer. Slightly break the duck bone and add to the stockpot, then add the duck meat that was removed from the leg and cook for 10 minutes. In a saucepan bring the coconut cream to a simmer. If using fresh coconut cream, please follow the instructions on the information on stocks and paste page 59.

Add paste to the coconut cream and cook for 12 minutes or until the curry has separated. Then loosen with the coconut milk stock, slowly adding the liquid at a time.

Add the palm sugar, duck meat, duck legs, and fish sauce. If wanting a dry curry, keep the liquid to a minimum; if wanting a wet curry, use most of the milk stock. Simmer for 15–20 minutes on a low heat, adding liquid when needed. Add the chili, basil and lychee.

Check the seasoning and adjust if needed. Top with the garnish and serve with a selection of sides.

Thai Food Sensation

SOUTHERN YELLOW CURRY OF BLUE EYE, SCALLOPS AND SHRIMP

GAENG LEUANG TA LAY

SERVES 4

Gaeng Leuang Ta Lay is a lovely sweet, sour and slight salty curry. The freshness of the lemongrass and the kaffir lime gives the curry a wonderful zing. The wonderful turmeric that gives a aroma of earthiness and the grachai that brings it all together. Any seafood can be used, I would not suggest any other protein other then seafood as the other proteins could over power the curry.

The paste
10 dried long red chilies, soaked, drained and de-seeded
pinch of salt
7 kaffir lime leaves
4 tablespoons lemongrass, sliced
10 slices galangal
12 slices fresh turmeric
3 tablespoons garlic, sliced
1 red shallots, slices
2 tablespoons cilantro roots
2 limes, zest
2 tablespoons cilantro seeds, roasted and pounded
1 teaspoon shrimp paste

The curry
450 g (15 oz) blue eye cod
12 scallops, whole
12 shrimp, tail on
250 ml (8 fl oz) coconut cream
430 ml (15 fl oz) coconut milk
750 ml (26 fl oz) vegetable stock (page 52)
2 lemongrass bulb, lightly bruised
5 kaffir lime leaves, torn
4 slices galangal
4 sliced turmeric
1 tablespoon grachi
12 cherry tomatoes
fish sauce to taste

3 tablespoons palm sugar
2 tablespoons tamarind water (page 41)
3 tablespoons lime juice

Garnish
1 handful sawtooth coriander
1 handful cilantro leaves
6 kaffir lime leaves, julienne very finely
green or red long chilies, julienne

To make the paste, follow the instructions on page 56.

Peel the shrimp, keeping the tails left on, clean the blue eye and cut into 4 slices. Clean the scallops by removing the outer membrane. Keep all the seafood in the fridge until needed.

In a saucepan bring the coconut milk and stock to the boil. In a saucepan bring the coconut cream to a simmer. If using fresh coconut cream please follow the instructions for cracking the cream (page 59). If using tinned coconut cream, this step is not necessary.

Once the coconut cream has split ,add the paste, simmer for 10 minutes on a very low heat allowing the oils to separate. Add the stock, simmer for 12 minutes. Add the palm sugar, fish sauce, lemongrass, kaffir lime, Galangal and fresh turmeric. (I like my yellow curry wet so I tend to use the whole liquid amount but if you like your curry dry, add less liquid.

Add the cherry tomatoes and the blue eye cod. Simmer for 7 minutes then add the scallops. Simmer for 4 minutes. Add the shrimp simmering for 4 minutes. Add the grachai and tamarind water, taste and adjust if needed.

Serve in a bowl, top with the garnish selection and serve with a selection of sides.

Thai Food Sensation

BEEF PANAENG CURRY

GENG PANAENG NEUA

SERVES 4

A Panaeng curry is one of the most popular in the Thai selection, full of richness with a base of salty and sweet flavors, perfumed with Thai basil. The background taste is one of roasted peanuts with the richness of coconut cream. The curry is normally made with beef but chicken and pork can be used.

Braising the chosen protein within the coconut milk will give the curry a rich, deep flavor and will allow the chosen protein to be tender and moist. If using chicken, cook on the bone as this will provide even more richness.

The paste
9 dried long red chilies, soaked, de-seeded and drained
pinch of salt
2 tablespoons galangal, chopped
1½ lemongrass stalks, chopped
2 kaffir lime leaves, sliced finely
1 teaspoon lime zest, chopped
2 large red shallots, grilled and chopped
6 garlic cloves, grilled
2 teaspoons cilantro root
1 teaspoon white pepper corn, and pounded

1 nutmeg, roasted and pounded
1 tablespoon cilantro seed, and pounded
6 tablespoons roasted nuts, pounded (page 29)
1 teaspoon shrimp paste

The curry
600 g (1⅓ lb) brisket or chuck steak, whole
1 L (32 fl oz) coconut milk (for braising)
500 ml (16 fl oz) water or chicken stock (page 51)

250 ml (8 fl oz) coconut cream
3 tablespoons palm sugar
4 kaffir lime leaves, torn
1 large handful Thai basil leaves
4 long red chilies, sliced in half
125 g (4 oz) roasted nuts (page 29)
3 tablespoons fish sauce

Garnish
3 kaffir lime leaves, julienne very finely
Thai basil
Thai chilies, sliced

Making the paste by following the directions on page 56.

In a stockpot bring the coconut milk and beef stock to the simmer. Add the beef to the milk and allow to simmer for 2 hours or until the meat is tender. Remove from the heat and allow the beef to cool in the liquid.

In a stockpot bring the coconut cream to a simmer. If using fresh coconut cream please follow the instructions for cracking the cream (page 59). If using tinned coconut cream, this step is not necessary.

Add the paste to the simmering coconut cream and allow to thicken slightly. Let the ingredients sweat off for 15 minutes before adding 3 cups of braising stock to the paste. If you prefer a dry curry, add less liquid; for a wet curry, add more liquid.

Add the palm sugar and the torn kaffir lime leaves. Season with the fish sauce. Taste and adjust if needed.

Remove the beef from the stock and slice thinly. Add the beef to the curry and allow to reheat.

Add most of the long red chilies reserving a small amount for garnish. Add the Thai basil and roasted peanuts. Simmer for 2 minutes then remove from the heat.

Spoon the curry into serving bowls and top with the garnish selections. Serve with jasmine rice (page 30) and roti (page 29).

JUNGLE CURRY OF SOFT PORK BONES

GAENG BPAA MUU

SERVES 3–4

Thai jungle curry is a very spicy curry from the north of Thailand. It is a curry that is bold in flavor, and is extremely spicy. Unlike most other curries found in the central plains or the south, northern curries have very little or no coconut cream added; they are stock based. The use of young bamboo, bitter greens and leaves are used. The base of this jungle curry is salty, bitter but overall spicy. The bitter element of the curry is mostly from the Thai pea eggplant and Thai apple.

The paste
4 dry red long chilies, soaked, de-seeded and drained
6 Thai bird's eye chilies
6 Thai scuds chilies
1 teaspoon salt
2 kaffir lime leaves
3 tablespoon lemongrass, chopped
4 slices galangal, chopped
1 large shallots, chopped
7 garlic cloves, chopped
6 cilantro root
2 tablespoon's grachai (wild ginger)
1 teaspoon shrimp paste

Pork bones
500 g (16 oz) soft pork bones, cooked and minced
3 L (5.25 pints) water

The curry
1 L (1¾ pints) of water or vegetable stock (see pak hun page 114)
250 g (8 oz) Thai pea eggplant
6 Thai apple eggplant, cut in half and deep fried until dark golden
½ bunch snake beans, sliced
250 g (8 oz) of young bamboo shoots, julienne

4 Thai scuds chilies (if wanting more spicy, bruise the chilies)
1 tablespoon palm sugar
4 tablespoons fish sauce
½ handful holy basil or Thai basil
2 tablespoons rice oil

Garnish
1 handful of sawtooth coriander
6 kaffir lime leaves, julienne very finely

In a large stockpot add the pork and water. Simmer for 3 hours until the pork bone is completely soft.then mince the pork by hand (keeping it rustic).

In a large stockpot add the oil and sweat off the paste for around 5 minutes. Add the minced pork. Cook the pork until the color changes. Add the pork stock or water and bring to a light simmer. Add the pea eggplant, deep fried apple eggplant, snake beans and palm sugar. Cook until pea eggplant is tender, but not too soft. They should retain a nice crunch when bitten into. Add the bamboo and the scud chilies. Warm through,then add the basil leaves and season with fish sauce. Taste and adjust if needed.

Top with the garnish selection and serve with jasmine rice (page 30).

Thai Food Sensation

GREEN CURRY OF BEEF, PEA EGGPLANTS AND DEEP FRIED QUAIL EGGS

GAENG KIEOW WAAN NEUA

SERVES 3–4

Green curry is a curry cooked and loved around the world. I love green curry; it's rich, spicy and can be cooked with different proteins. The best green curry I have had in Thailand was at a restaurant, *Bplaa Tuu* all the way down near Hau hin. This green curry had little pea eggplants that had a wonderful bitterness when bitten into. It was highly flavored with fresh Thai basil and creamy fresh coconut milk spooned over the top. Quail eggs add a wonderful creamy feel to the curry. Salted duck egg can be used as an alternative.

125 g (4 oz) green curry paste (page 60)

The paste
600 g (20 oz) chunk stake or brisket
1 L (32 fl oz) coconut milk
1 L (32 fl oz) water or chicken stock (page 51)
375 ml (12 fl oz) coconut cream

4 tablespoons palm sugar
8 whole Thai green chilies
125 g (4 oz) pea eggplants
125 g (4 oz) green snake beans, cut 2 cm (¾ in) long
14 fresh quail eggs or tinned, fried until dark golden
6 kaffir lime leaves, torn

6 kaffir lime leaves, julienne very finely
3 tablespoons fish sauce or to taste
2 handfuls Thai basil leaves

Garnish
Thai basil
Thai chilies, julienne

To make the paste, follow the instructions on page 56.

Bring the coconut milk and the stock or water to the simmer and braise the beef for 2 hours or until tender. Allow the meat to cool in the braising liquid. Keep the liquid. In a saucepan bring the coconut cream to a simmer.

If using fresh coconut cream please follow the instructions for cracking the cream (page 59). If using tinned coconut cream, this step is not necessary.

Once the cream is cracked or simmering, add in the paste and cook out for 10 minutes. Pour 1½ cup of beef braising liquid into the saucepan bring to a simmer. Add the pea eggplants and cook for 4 minutes, then add the kaffir lime leaves, snake beans, palm sugar and fresh chilies. Simmer for 8 minutes. If you want a dry curry add less stock, if wanting a wet curry add more stock until the thickness of your liking. Slice the beef and add to the curry, season with fish sauce – taste, adjust if needed. Turn the head off and then add the basil leaves and the fried quail eggs. (The quail eggs should be golden brown.)

MUSSAMAN CHICKEN CURRY WITH SWEET PINEAPPLE

GAENG MUSSAMAN GAI

SERVES 3–4

With the richness of all the spices, this curry has smooth after finish of sweet pineapple which gives this curry a very different taste and texture to all others. The richness of the roasted peanuts and the starchy potatoes work hand in hand. Mussaman can be made with any choice of protein.

The paste
10 long dried red chilies, soaked, de-seeded, drained
large pinch of salt
1 tablespoon garlic, grilled
5 small shallots, grilled
1 tablespoon galangal, grilled
1 tablespoon lemongrass, sliced, grilled
2 tablespoon cilantro roots, grilled
1 teaspoon cumin seeds, roasted and pounded
1 tablespoon cilantro seed roasted and pounded
1 teaspoon white pepper corns, roasted and pounded

½ nutmeg, roasted and pounded
3 cardamom pods, roasted and pounded
2 bay leaves ground, roasted and pounded
4 cloves, roasted and pounded
1 cassia bark, roasted and pounded
125 g (4 oz) peanuts, roasted and pounded
1 tablespoon shrimp paste, fresh

The curry
5 chicken legs, each cut into 3 pieces
250 ml (8 fl oz) coconut cream
750 ml (26 fl oz) water or chicken stock (page 51)
500 ml (16 fl oz) coconut milk

2 tablespoon pickled ginger
125 g (4 oz) roasted peanuts, pound lightly
5 tablespoons palm sugar
4 tablespoons fish sauce
3 large potatoes, peel, quartered
6 red shallots, cut in half
½ pineapple, peeled and diced
5 tablespoons tamarind water
rice oil for deep frying

Garnish
roasted peanuts
julienne Thai chilies
fried shallots

To make the paste, follow the instructions on page 56. In a large wok or deep fryer heat the oil, add the chicken pieces and fry until golden, take out and place onto absorbent paper. Deep fry the shallots until just golden, take out and place onto absorbent paper. Bring the coconut milk and the water or stock to the boil and then add the Chicken, Braise for 30 to 40 minutes or until the chicken is tender. Turn off the heat, allow the chicken to cool inside the liquid.

In a saucepan, cook the potatoes, starting in cold water, once the potatoes are soft on the out side but still just hard in the middle take them of the heat, strain and cool. Take out the chicken, strain the liquid into a reserved bowl, do not throw out the braising liquid. In a saucepan bring the coconut cream to a simmer. If using fresh coconut cream please follow the instructions for cracking the cream (page 57). If using tinned coconut cream, this step is not necessary.

Add the paste to the cracked or simmering coconut cream and stir until very well combined. Simmer the paste for 10 minutes allowing the oils to separate. Add in the braising stock, if needing more add more. Simmer for 6 minutes. Add the palm sugar, tamarind water, peanuts and ginger. Season with fish sauce, taste and adjust if needed. Add the chicken, potatoes, shallots and sweet pineapple. Allow the ingredients to heat through. Top with the garnish and serve immediately.

DRY RED SHRIMP AND BUG CURRY

CHUU CHII GUNG GANG

SERVES 2–3

Chuu Chii is mostly cooked with seafood, such as lobster, scallops, clams, mussels and fish. This curry is very much like a red curry; the only difference is that this curry is fried in oil not coconut cream and it is stock based. Flavored with kaffir lime leaves and Thai basil, it has a salty, sweet and rich base.

The paste
12 dried red chilies, soaked, de-seeded, drained
large pinch of salt
2 tablespoons galangal, chopped
4 tablespoons lemongrass stalks, chopped
3 teaspoon kaffir lime zest, sliced
3 small shallots, chopped
6 garlic cloves, chopped
4 cilantro roots
2 teaspoons shrimp paste

The curry
450 g (15 oz) prawns, shelled and de-veined, tail left on
500 g (16 oz) bug tail flesh, shelled, sliced into 4 cm (1 in) slices
113 g (6 oz) curry paste
10 kaffir lime leaves, torn
2 tablespoons palm sugar
2 tablespoons fish sauce
125 ml (4 fl oz) water or vegetable stock (page 52)
1 handful Thai basil leaves

7 fresh chilies, sliced
4 kaffir lime leaves, julienne very finely
2 tablespoons rice oil

Garnish
kaffir lime leaves, julienne
Thai basil
Thai chilies

To make the paste, follow the instructions on page 56.

In a second saucepan add the oil and bring to a medium heat, add in the curry paste and fry on a low heat for 10 minutes. Add the bug tails and shrimp, mix well to incorporated into the curry paste, add the stock or water and simmer lightly. Add in the palm sugar and fish sauce, followed by the fresh chilies (reserve a small amount for garnish) and torn kaffir lime leaves.

Turn the flam to high and quickly fry all together, Add in the Thai basil, mix well.

Serve topped with the garnish selection and a side of jasmine rice (page 30).

CHICKEN AND GALANGAL SOUP

DTOM KHAA GAI

SERVES 4

Dtom Khaa is one of the most known Thai soups, known for its sour, spicy and rich coconut cream broth. This simple soup is packed full of flavor. It is mostly made with chicken or seafood. The lemongrass and kaffir lime leaves gives freshness and the fresh chilies provide heat and spice.

4 chicken thighs, bone in
750 ml (1½ pints) chicken stock
  (page 51)
375 ml (12½ fl oz) coconut milk
375 ml (12½ fl oz) coconut cream
pinch of salt
2 teaspoons palm sugar
3 lemongrass stalks, trimmed

1 red shallot
4 cilantro roots
4 Thai chilies
11 slices galangal
6 kaffir lime leaves, torn
200 g (6 oz) oyster mushroom, torn
  into strips

6 kaffir lime leaves, julienne very
  finely
4–5 green Thai chilies
1 handful cilantro leaves
4 tablespoons lime juice
4 tablespoons fish sauce

In a sauce pot combined the stock and coconut milk. Bring to the boil, then add the chicken thighs and cook on a low simmer for around 30 minutes of until the flesh is just coming away from the bone.

Add the sugar and the fish sauce. Bruise the lemongrass, galangal, cilantro roots, Thai chilies and shallots in a mortar and pestle. Add this to the stock and allow to simmer for 4 minutes.

Add the torn kaffir lime leaves, oyster mushrooms and cilantro root. Simmer for 3 minutes then take off the heat.

Place 1 tablespoon of lime juice and 1 tablespoon of fish sauce into each bowl. Ladle the soup into each bowl, top the soup with additional kaffir lime leaves, chilies or cilantro leaves. Serve with jasmine rice (page 30)

BEEF NOODLE SOUP

KUAY TIAW REUA

SERVES 4

Kuay Tiaw Reua is a very popular soup in Thailand. It is found on every corner of every region of the kingdom. The richness, freshness and aroma are amazing. This soup is well worth the effect it takes to make. The sides are very important to *Kuay Tiaw Reua* as the seasoning takes place at the table, not in the kitchen. Guests determine the flavors to their liking. Any rice noodle can be eaten with *Kuay Tiaw Reua* and you can choose beef, pork, chicken or all three.

The stock
4 L (7 pints) chicken stock (page 51)
4 tablespoons sugar
1 teaspoon salt
180 ml (6 fl oz) Thai soy sauce
2 tablespoons black soy sauce
180 ml (6 fl oz) sweet soy sauce
1 bunch cilantro root
2 shallots, grilled
4 garlic cloves, grilled
1 cassia bark, roasted
2 star anise, roasted
1 teaspoon cilantro seeds, roasted
2 tablespoon galangal, sliced
2 lemongrass stalks, sliced
1 pandan leaf, tied into a knot
½ bunch Chinese celery, chopped
1 tablespoon black peppercorn

The soup
500 g (16 oz) brisket
300 g (10 oz) beef tenderloin or scotch fillet, sliced very finely
400 ml (13 fl oz) beef or pork blood (optional)
1 packet beef balls, cut in half
400 g (13 oz) linguine-shaped rice noodles, soaked in lukewarm water for 15 minutes.
1 bunch morning glory or water spinach, chopped

Garnish
2 handfuls Thai basil leaves
1 bunch cilantro leaves
1 bunch spring onions, sliced
bean sprouts, washed and drained

Sides
lemon wedges
fish sauce
white sugar
soaked chilies in fish sauce (page 44)
vinegar soaked chilies (page 45)
chili powder
fried garlic (page 27)

In a large stockpot add the stock and bring to a boil. Add all other ingredients for the stock. Add the brisket then simmer with the lid on for 1½ to 2 hours or until tender. Remove the brisket. Sieve the stock through muslin cloth. Pour the stock back into the stockpot and bring to a light simmer. Skim any oil or scum off the top. Tear the beef brisket into strips, set aside. Have all the ingredients ready to go in their own bowls. Once ready, heat a stockpot with water and bring to a high boil. Have the beef stock simmering and have all your serving bowls ready in a line.

Take 4 containers and add equal parts of raw tenderloin, beef brisket and beef balls. Take 4 new containers and add equal parts of noodles, morning glory or water spinach and bean sprouts (although eaten fresh I find is more enjoyable). Before cooking, make sure your table is ready with the side dishes and that nothing is missing. It's very important not to let the noodles sit in the stock as the noodles will suck up all the liquid.

Fill a wire cooking basket with the container of noodles. Place into the boiling water and slowly move the basket around for 30 seconds. Remove, strain the water and place into your first bowl. Very quickly place container of raw tenderloin into the wire basket. This time place it into the simmering stock for 30 seconds then transfer it into the bowl with the noodles. Pour the blood into a ladle and sit in the stock briefly to heat slightly. Pour into the bowl. Take a ladle of stock and pour over the bowl.

Serve the first bowl immediately. Start on the second serving and repeat until everyone is served. Enjoy with guests deciding on their own garnish and sides.

Thai Food Sensation

SOUR ISAAN SOFT PORK BONE SOUP

TOM SAEP MUU

SERVES 4

Tom Saep Muu is a rich, sour, spicy and fresh soup. The lemongrass, kaffir lime leaves and galangal give the broth a zing and tartness. Soft bones are very popular but beef can also be used. The use of offal is also important as the offal gives richness but can be left out if not to your taste.

The soup broth should be salty, slightly sour and spicy. I like my *Tom Saep* more sour than others. I suggest adding a small amount of lime and tasting as you go to find your limit, but in saying this the soup does need a good amount of sourness to it.

The soup
1½ kg (2½ lbs) soft pork bones, washed and sliced
5 L (175 fl oz) chicken stock (p 51)
6 slices galangal
4 lemongrass, Sliced
1 red shallot, grilled
8 kaffir lime leaves, torn
1 bunch cilantro root
1 teaspoon black pepper, roasted and pounded
3 garlic cloves, pounded

2 tablespoons palm sugar
1 large red chili
5 long dried red chilies, roasted and pounded
125 g (4 oz) tripe
125 ml (4 fl oz) tamarind water (page 41)
125 g (4 oz) pork offal of each heart, liver and kidney (optional)
40 ml (1½ fl oz) lime juice
40 ml (1½ fl oz) fish sauce

Garnish
4 kaffir lime leaves, julienne
1 handful sawtooth coriander, torn
1 handful cilantro leaves, torn
4 dried red chilies, roasted and pounded lightly
scallion (spring onion), sliced
2 Thai chilies, bruised
1 lemongrass, purple part only sliced very finely

Dice or slice the offal to your preference. Prepare the garnish selection and set aside.

To make the stock, heat the grill and cook the pork bones until nicely golden. In a large stockpot, bring the stock to the boil, add the pork bones and tripe and bring to a simmer. Add the galangal, lemongrass, grilled shallot, garlic, chilies and pepper. Simmer for 2 to 3 hours covered with a lid. Once the pork and the tripe are tender, add the kaffir lime leaves, cilantro root, fish sauce, tamarind water and palm sugar.

Bring the stock quickly to the boil, turn to a simmer, then add the offal, lime juice and fish sauce. Simmer for 3 minutes. Turn off the heat.

Serve in required bowls, top with garnish selection and serve with jasmine rice (page 30). You might want add all your garnish selection to the bowl beforehand, then pour the hot stock over the garnish. Mix well before serving. Serve with garnish and jasmine rice (page 30).

PORK HOCK WITH CHINESE FIVE SPICE AND BOILED EGG

KAAO KHA MUU

SERVES 6

Kaao Kha Muu is not considered a soup but more of a Thai stew found all over Thailand and in the streets of Bangkok. The rich smell of Chinese five spice fills the air—the dark rich broth that is so balanced in elements of sweet and salty. The stew is quite easy to put together but takes time to cook. Steamed bok choy or pickled mustard make a terrific side. Pickled mustard (pickled cabbage) can be found in many Asian supermarkets.

The paste
1 whole garlic bulb, skin on
5 cilantro roots, washed
3 tablespoons galangal, sliced
3–4 teaspoons five spice powder
1 tablespoon white pepper, roasted

The broth
3 pork hocks, cut in half (ask your butcher to do this)
4 L (7 pints) water or chicken stock
125 ml (4 fl oz) black Thai soy sauce
250 ml (8 fl oz) thin Thai soy sauce
180 ml (6 fl oz) Thai oyster sauce
180 ml (6 fl oz) Shao Hsing wine
125 g (4 oz) palm sugar
4 Pandan leaves, tied into a knot

Garnish
8 eggs, boiled for 8 minutes
3 whole bok choy, cut in half
pickled mustard

Sides
jasmine rice (page 30)
vinegar soaked chilies (page 45)

Turn on a gas flame (barbecue or stove) and hold the pork hock with tongs over the flame to burn any hairs that are still on the hock.

Turn on the grill and place the pork hock onto an oven tray. Grill for 40 minutes to remove fat and oil.

Place the garlic bulb straight onto the flame (or grill) until the skin burns. Cut in half and pound.

Add all the other ingredients for the paste and to a paste consistency.

In a large stockpot, add the water or stock, the paste and bring to a light boil. Once the pork hocks are golden, add to the stock. Add all of the liquids, palm sugar and pandan leaves and simmer for 3½ hours or until the pork is just falling off the bone.

Peel the eggs and place into the stock to simmer for 30 minutes (I like my eggs just boiled and not simmered in the stock—so if you're like me, leave them out of the stock. Slice the eggs in half and set aside.)

If using the pickled mustard, chop the cabbage into bite size strips, place into a small pot and top with stock, simmer until tender and rich in color. If serving with steamed bok choy, place into a Thai steamer and steam for 6 minutes.

Remove the pork from the stock and gently remove the pork meat and skin. Cut the pork into around thin cuts (serve with the skin).

To serve, spoon some rice onto the middle of each plate. Flatten slightly. Top the rice with the pork. Place the eggs to one side of the plate and the bok choy or pickled mustard (cabbage) to the other. Pour the broth over making sure that there is a small bath of broth on the bottom of the plate. Serve with vinegar soaked chilies.

SPICY SHRIMP SOUR SOUP

THOM YUM GONG

SERVES 4

Thom Yum is a very popular dish, one that comes in many different styles and flavors. Sweet, spicy, salty and sour a wonderful soup that is enriched with a fresh broth. Making the Thom yum paste is a lot of fun, but more importantly the paste gives so much more flavor then a jar or tin of paste would.

Thom Yum paste (page 31)
3 L (5 pints) vegetable stock
(page 52)
2 tomatoes, each cut into 4
2 cilantro roots
6 kaffir lime leaves, torn
2 lemongrass stalks, sliced
6 slices galangal
2 red shallots, sliced
5 bird's eye chilies

2 tablespoons tamarind water
(page 41)
2 tablespoons chili jam (page 40)
1 tablespoon palm sugar
1–1.5 kg (2–3½ lbs) tiger prawns
1 handful oyster mushrooms, torn
roughly
2 tablespoon of rice oil

Sides
1 handful cilantro leaves
3 tablespoons lime, juice
1–2 tablespoons fish sauce
6 long red chilies, roasted
5 Thai chilies, bruised
1 lemongrass stalk, purple part only
sliced finely
handful sawtooth coriander
jasmine rice (page 30)

To make the paste, follow the instructions on page 56.

Peel and devein the shrimp, leaving the head on. Keep the shells for stock.

In a stockpot add the stock and bring to a boil. Add the shrimp shells and cook for 10 minutes before shifting the shells out.

In a new stockpot add the oil. Heat then add the paste allowing the paste to simmer and darken slightly. Add the stock and bring to a simmer and allow flavors to combine for 10 minutes. Add the lemongrass, galangal, chilies, red shallots, kaffir lime leaves, tomato and cilantro root. Bring to a boil and then turn down to a simmer for 5 minutes. Add the shrimp, oyster mushrooms, tamarind water, chili jam and palm sugar. Cook for 5 minutes or until the shrimp are just cooked.

Squeeze the lime juice and add the fish sauce to each bowl. Add the other garnishes. Top with the stock and shrimp. Stir and serve immediately with jasmine rice and sides.

Nightlife
in
Thailand

The nightlife in Bangkok is a chaotic affair, the streets are bustling with every possible vehicle and the footpaths are a traffic jam of feet and vendors cooking and selling night street food. The night markets are in overdrive with tourists looking for bargains. Walking past the same area in the day feels completely different from that of the night. Shops that were closed in the morning and the afternoon are now open, whisky bars and pubs are all playing music and serving cold beer straight from the taps. It's a second world to that of the day life and it's an unbelievable feeling walking the streets of Bangkok looking at all the magical scenery and hearing and seeing the Thai people all in action.

The night is all about eating with the night weather being the best of the day. Red coals in the pit are brightly burning and the nightlife is becoming a food paradise with the main attraction being that of the freshly-caught seafood that sits on display waiting to be chosen, to then be grilled or steamed in front of your eyes.

It's so easy to sit on the footpath on a tiny blue plastic stool and eat until you're stuffed and then smash down a few glasses of whisky with wonderful company and views.

Thailand's beauty of old and rustic comes alive in the night with the lights shining off the old buildings and the surroundings. There is a true culture within Thailand that can be seen from morning to night; the food culture and the social culture of that of the Thai people. Their life is not about waking up going to work, being stressed out to the max trying to fight for a bigger pay salary then rush home and watch TV. It's about life, living, food, friendship and most importantly respect and love of their country.

Most of the food that is served during the night is stir-fried, deep-fried or grilled. For Bangkok, the famous Chinatown is one of the busiest locations and food provinces. A trip to Chinatown is a must for anyone wanting to eat the most awesome stir-fries, soups and broths. My suggestion is to find the busiest restaurant, sit down and just ask the waiter to serve you whatever they suggest. It's a guessing game, one that might be tasteful or a challenge, but either way it's fun. A bowl of chicken offal soup might be placed down or a bowl of boiled tongue or a curry of chicken feet. Whatever it is, do try it. You may well find a new taste sensation. Think of it as an awesome adventure and that you have taken a step to trying some thing new—this is what life is all about.

The nightlife in Bangkok holds many attractions and enjoyment. For many, it's the best part of the day, due to the streets being so busy with people and traffic. It's a great feeling to be in the crowd and to feel the rush and excitement. Every city has a different experience. Take for instance, Pattaya. It is the city of girls, lady boys and go-go bars. It is known as the party location of Thailand, the most populated tourist destination due to its nightlife and other attractions.

The countryside of Thailand is a lot different from Bangkok or any tourist destination. The Thai people from the country regions will head to the market early in the afternoon and buy their ingredients for supper, or pick up an easy meal for the family. Once it's dinnertime, all will seat together and eat. A bomb fire could be used for added heat. The nights are peaceful, the stars are extremely bright and the sound of the wind can be heard brushing against the banana leaves. The countryside is so relaxing and quiet that a walk around the town or a bike ride is a must. The markets close earlier and the shops are all locked by 8 pm with most families watching their favorite drama on TV or heading to bed for another long, hot day in the fields.

Thailand night meals are usually cooked to order dishes and Thai desserts. They are mostly wok cooked; a mixture of Chinese and Thai cuisines. The streets are filled with the sound of sizzling and the banging of the woks being tossed. The dishes are mostly *Ahaan Jaan Diaw* (one-plated meal) but dishes can be ordered and placed onto the table and shared if you wish. The most famous night dish would have to be *Pat Bai Grapao*, a stir-fry of minced protein of choice, chilies and basil served with a spoon of rice and a fried egg soaked in fish sauce. *Pat Bai Grapao* is a spicy meal that is sweetened by holy basil, although Thai basil can be used.

The kitchen is an open footpath with large gas bottles sitting around a cart that is housing most of the ingredients. The arrangement of different dishes that are served along the streets of Thailand means that you will be able to find many different dishes to try. Stir-fried clams with chili jam, stir-fried seafood, grilled rock lobster and fresh scallops are all waiting to be bought. Either grilled on red hot coals or steamed then served with a spicy nahrm—the decision is yours. The most amazing crispy pork belly can be seen hanging through the windows of vendors lining Chinatown's main strip. Peking ducks also hang in shop windows.

The night dishes are quick to make and are easy to put together due to the time needed to quickly serve you and then the next person in line. Plastic tables and stools litter the footpath. Hungry Thai people sit screaming over each over with whisky in hand. Every Tok Tok and taxi owner is asking every foreigner walking past if they would like to explore the city.

The Thais love their desserts. Dessert vendors are serving the creamiest, lush coconut sugar delights, poured into plastic bags and filled with tapioca jellies of different colors and shapes. Deep-fried Chinese bread is not just a breakfast favorite but also a popular dessert with Pandas custard. You'll find banana fritters layered with sesame seeds, mango and sticky rice, bananas stewed in salted coconut milk, taro cake, roti with condensed milk and white sugar or roti stuffed with egg and banana fillings. Fresh fruit can also be found in abundance.

The Thai dessert selection is elegant, skillful and well balanced with sweetness, lightness, saltiness and also richness. Whatever the time, Thailand is always awake serving the best savory wonders and sweet gems that will for fill any hungry hawker or sweet tooth.

COOKED TO ORDER

MUSSELS WITH CHILI JAM

HOI MALAENG PUU NAHM PRIK PAO

SERVES 2

This dish is normally cooked on the streets of Bangkok made with clams, perfumed with Thai basil and enriched with chili jam that give sweetness, saltiness and sharpness. I like to garnish with lemongrass, kaffir lime and also julienne chili although this is not a garnish you would find on the streets.

1 kg (32 oz) mussels (or clams), cleaned and beards removed
1 shallot, finely sliced
3 garlic cloves, finely sliced
4 kaffir lime leaves, torn
1 teaspoon palm sugar
2 tablespoons fish sauce

1 handful of Thai basil
4–5 tablespoon chili jam
splash of water
2 tablespoons rice oil

Garnish
1 long red chili, julienne

2 kaffir lime leaves, julienne
1 handful cilantro leaves
1 lemongrass, purple part only, sliced finely
1 tablespoon fried shallots (page 27)
jasmine rice (page 30)

Clean the mussels by scrubbing them with a clean steel wool. Remove beards and rinse well. Heat the wok to a very high heat. Add the oil, shallots and garlic then quickly add the mussels and give a very good stir. Allow muscles to open completely before adding the chili jam and a splash of water. Mix well. Add the palm sugar and the fish sauce. When all is combined well, add the kaffir lime leaves and the Thai basil. Slightly heat the basil leaves then turn off the heat.

Serve with the garnish and a selection of sides.

Thai Food Sensation

CRISPY PORK BELLY WITH MORNING GLORY

PAT PAK BONG MUU GROP

SERVES 3

This dish is a favorite. I suggest heading down to your local Chinese restaurant to pick up some crispy pork belly. This can be served as a side or main dish.

- 1 kg (32 oz) pork belly, sliced into chunks, 2½ cm (1 inch) thick
- 1 large bunches morning glory
- 1 tablespoon garlic
- 2 tablespoons oyster sauce
- 1 tablespoon light soy sauce
- 1 tablespoon fish sauce
- splash of water
- 5 Thai chilies, bruised
- 2 cilantro roots, sliced
- 2 tablespoons oil
- pinch of sugar
- jasmine rice (page 30)
- vinegar soaked chilies (page 45)

Heat a large wok until it begins to smoke. Add the oil then the garlic, cilantro root and chilies. Sweat off quickly. Add the morning glory, tossing and stirring quickly as the cooking should to be fast. Add the liquids, sugar and the pork belly. Turn off the heat.

Serve with jasmine rice (page 30) , chilies and a selection of sides.

GRILLED SALTED RED SNAPPER WITH LEMONGRASS

BPLAA PHAO KLEUA

SERVES 2

Bplaa Phao Kleua is found all over Thailand grilling over hot coals. Snakefish is the most popular fish to use. The scales are left on then covered with a heavy blanket of salt that protects the fish not just from burning but also helps to retain its moisture. The scales allow the fish to adsorb the flavor of salt but does not allow too much salt to penetrate. It also allows the salt to stick to the fish. The salted crust is then removed with the skin and only the flesh is eaten. The fish is accompanied by an array of fresh vegetables, white noodles or rice paper and a spicy sauce. The best way to eat this dish is to take a small amount of fish, then take a cup of lettuce and an arrangement of other ingredients. Roll every thing together and eat in one mouthful.

425 g (15 oz) table salt
2 lemongrass stalks, bruised
1 baby red snapper, approximately 1
    kg (32 oz), gutted, scales left on

Sides
fresh cucumbers
fresh chilies
iceberg lettuce
western mint
Vietnamese mint
cilantro leaves
any white noodle

rice paper, optional

Optional sides
roast banana pepper relish (page 37)
seafood dipping sauce (page 35)
soaked chili in fish sauce (page 44)
sticky rice (page 31)

Heat the coals to red hot, allow the coals to became gray before cooking.

Make the dressings and have the side selection ready.

Stuff the fish with the lemongrass. Cover the whole fish with salt from head to tail. Place onto the grill and cook for around 10 minutes each side, depending on the size of the fish.

Place the fish onto a plate. Serve with a selection of sides.

Thai Food Sensation

STIR-FRIED CHILI BASIL WITH CHICKEN

GAI PAT BAI GRAPAO

SERVES 2

Pat Bai Grapao is the most popular dish on the streets of Thailand. Any protein can be used; in this dish I am using chicken. This popular dish is renown for its fried egg that sits on top of the rice. It is spicy and sweet from the Holy basil; if you cant find holy basil use Thai basil. The egg is shallow fried in oil, not flipped. The oil gives it puffiness and it is only slightly cooked on top.

- 400 g (13 oz) chicken breast, hand minced
- 6 garlic cloves, semi pounded
- 5 Thai chilies, semi pounded
- 4 tablespoons oyster sauce

- 1 tablespoon soy sauce
- 2 tablespoons fish sauce
- splash of water
- 1 tablespoon white sugar
- 1 handful of holy basil or Thai Basil

- 2 eggs
- 2 dried chilies, broken
- 3 tablespoons rice oil

Heat the wok with the oil. Once the oil is smoking, crack the two eggs into the wok. Cook for 5 minutes. Take out and set aside.

Keep the wok on high. Add the chilies and garlic and cook until just golden. Add the chicken mince and keep moving around the wok. Once the chicken is just cooked, add in the liquids, sugar and dried chilies. Cook until chicken is completely cooked then add the holy basil or Thai basil.

Place a spoonful of jasmine rice (page 30) onto each plate. Spoon the dish onto the plate but not over the rice. Top the rice with the egg. Serve with a side of soaked chilies in fish sauce (page 45).

CHICKEN PAD THAI

PAT THAI GAI

SERVES 2

Pat (Pad) Thai is the beacon of Thai cuisine outside Thailand. Who has not tried Pat Thai before? I have not met anyone to date who has not. This sweet, sour and slight spicy noodle is heaven when made well. A tip: It's very important to slice the chicken breast very finely as the cooking period needs to be very fast.

Tamarind dressing
2 tablespoons tamarind water (page 41)
2 tablespoons fish sauce
1 tablespoon sweet soy sauce
3 tablespoons palm sugar
2 tablespoons water

Stir-fry
200 g (7 oz) chicken breast, sliced very thinly
375 g (12 oz) Pat Thai noodles, soaked 20 minutes, drained
200 g (7 oz) fried bean curd
3 garlic cloves, sliced finely
1 Shallot, Sliced finely
1 egg
½ bunch Chinese chives
2 tablespoons rice oil

Garnish
1 handful Chinese chives
1 handful deep fried peanuts, semi pounded
1 handful roasted dried long red chilies, semi pounded
1 key lime, wedge
1 handful bean sprouts
1 banana leaf for base, optional

Side
vinegar soaked chilies (page 45), optional

Combine the palm sugar and the water. Place in the microwave for 2 minutes. Be careful when taking out as it will be hot.

Add the tamarind water, sweet soy sauce, fish sauce and sugar syrup together and mix well. Set aside.

Heat the wok to a high heat. Add the oil, garlic and shallot. Sweat off quickly then add the egg and fry until the base is golden. Flip and cook the bottom to golden. Using the wok spoon, break the egg into pieces. Add the chicken and cook for 5 minutes or just until the chicken is sealed then add the noodles. Fry the noodles for 2 minutes, moving the noodles now and then. Add in the tamarind dressing, bean curd and chives. Mix quickly to incorporate. Once the noodles are coated well and the chicken cooked, turn off the heat.

If using the banana leaf, place on the bottom of the plate. Plate the Pat Thai in the middle.

Place the vinegar soaked chilies of the side with the garnish selection.

Keep everything separated and in a neat pile besides the bean sprouts that go on the top of the noodles.

PORK BELLY SAUTÉED IN RED CURRY PASTE

PAHT PEHT MUU

SERVES 2

I remember being in a little restaurant in Mukdahan, a province west of Nakhon Phanom overlooking the Mekong river. The cook was an older lady who had years of experience cooking *Paht Peht Muu*. The flavor was exquisite.

The paste
650 g (20 oz) pork belly, sliced thin
4–5 tablespoons of red curry paste
2–3 teaspoons palm sugar
2 long red chilies, sliced
5 kaffir lime leaves, julienne finely

½ bunch snake beans, sliced into 2
    cm (1 inch) lengths
2 tablespoons fish sauce
3 tablespoons water or stock
1 handful of holy basil or Thai basil
2 tablespoons rice oil

3 kaffir lime leaves, julienne very
    finely
1 long red chili, julienne very finely

Make red curry paste as per instructions (page 56).

In a bowl add the pork and the red curry. Allow too marinate to 2 hours.

Heat the wok to a super high heat. Add the oil then the pork. Stir and quickly fry off the pork and the paste before adding the stock or water. Allow the pork to simmer until cooked, around 8 minutes. Add more stock if needed to make sure the paste has a loose consistency.

Add the palm sugar, long red chilies, kaffir lime leaves and the snake beans. Simmer for 4 minutes. Add the fish sauce and the holy basil or Thai basil. Turn the heat off.

Place the *Paht Peht* onto a plate, top with julienne kaffir lime leaves, chili and serve with jasmine rice (page 30) .

Thai Food Sensation

MUSHROOM WITH PORK, BOK CHOY AND WHITE PEPPER

PAHT HEHT SAI MUU

SERVES 2

Paht Heht is a very simple dish that takes no time at all to cook, It's a wonderful meal or side dish that has a texture and flavor. Enkoi mushrooms and black fungi are available at many Asian supermarkets.

- 250 g (8 oz) scotch fillet, sliced finely
- 2 tablespoon garlic, slice finely
- 2 tablespoon of shallots, sliced
- 1 bok choy, sliced
- 2 handfuls oyster mushrooms, torn

- 2 handfuls Enkoi mushrooms, sliced
- 2 handful black fungi, sliced
- 3 tablespoons fish sauce
- ½ teaspoon white pepper
- 60 ml (2 fl oz) water

- 2 tablespoons rice oil
- 2 spring onions, sliced
- fried shallots (page 27)
- fried garlic (page 27)

Heat the wok to a very high heat. Add the oil, shallot, garlic, bok choy and the pork. Quickly fry off then add the mushrooms and white pepper. Allow to cook for 5 minutes keeping the wok moving. Add the water and the fish sauce. Take off the heat.

Place on a plate, top with garnish selection and serve with side selection and jasmine rice (page 30).

Thai Food Sensation

STEAMED WHOLE BABY BARRAMUNDI WITH CHILI, GARLIC AND LIME

BPLAA NEUNG MANAO

SERVES 4

Bplaa Neung Manao is a very healthy meal, one that looks amazing and tastes awesome. It can be a meal on its own but it is normally served to be shared with other dishes. Grachai is a type of ginger available in many Asian supermarkets.

1 large baby barramundi, whole and
    cleaned
4 slices galangal, semi pounded
2 lemongrass stalks, semi pounded
4 Thai red chilies, semi pounded
1 tablespoon grachai, semi pounded
3 cilantro roots, semi pounded
4 garlic cloves, semi pounded
2 tablespoons fish sauce

4 tablespoons lime juice
1 teaspoon white sugar
1 banana leaf

Garnish
3 spring onions
1 handful cilantro leaves
2 long red chilies, julienne very finely
fried garlic (page 27)

Sides
seafood dipping sauce (page 35)
roast tomato relish (page 36) or
roast banana pepper relish (page 37)
soaked chilies in fish sauce (page 44)
sticky rice (page 31)
fresh arrangement of herbs
fresh arrangement of vegetables

Mix all the pounded ingredients together and stuff into the cavity of the fish. Set aside.

Put the fish on a plate and pour over the liquids. Cover with silver foil making a few small holes. Place into the steamer and cover with a lid. Steam for 16 minutes for until the fish is cooked.

Gently lay the fish on a new plate. Keep the juices and pour over the fish. Top with the garnish selection and serve with a side selection of your choice.

FRIED CRISPY PORK WITH CHINESE BROCCOLI

PAT KANAA MUU GROP

SERVES 2

Pat Kanaa Muu Grop **is a super quick and easy dish to put together and is wonderful for the busy person looking for a wonderful meal but a easy process.**

500 g (16 oz) roast pork, shop
  brought and sliced
4 Thai chili, semi pounded
3 cloves garlic, semi pounded

2 bunches bok choy, blanched
2 tablespoons oyster sauce
2 tablespoons light soy sauce
2 tablespoons water

1 tablespoon palm sugar
pinch of salt
2 tablespoons rice oil

Heat the wok to a very high heat. Add the oil, chilies and garlic and sweat off until just golden.

Add the bok choy and the pork. Mix well. Add the liquids, palm sugar and salt.

Serve with jasmine rice (page 30) and a side selection of your choice.

Thai Food Sensation

PORK FRIED RICE WITH CRABMEAT AND CHILI JAM

KAOW PHAT MUU BPUU PRIK PAO

SERVES 2

200 g (7 oz) roasted pork shoulder, sliced
125 g (4 oz) crabmeat
3 garlic cloves, sliced
1 shallot, diced finely
1 long red chili, sliced

1 egg
680 g (22 oz) jasmine rice (page 19)
4–5 tablespoon chili jam (page 35)
2 tablespoon white sugar
2 tablespoon fish sauce
1 teaspoon sugar

2 tablespoon rice oil
1 handful spring onion, sliced
½ handful of cilantro leaves
vinegar soaked chilies (page 45) or
sweet chili sauce (page 42)
cucumber

Thai fried rice is a great quick meal, tasty meal that I love. It is wonderful to have fried rice once a week and use up any leftovers you might have laying around.

Heat the wok to a very high temperature. Add the oil and when it begins to smoke, crack the egg into the middle of the wok. Cook for 1 minute then flip the egg and then slide the egg to the side.

Add the shallot, chili and garlic. Allow the garlic, chili and shallots to golden then break the egg into small pieces.

Add the pork and the crabmeat and cook for 30 seconds. Add the chili jam, sugar and fish sauce. Mix well. Add the rice and mix. Fry the rice until you have a semi-dry texture.

Place into a bowl and top with garnish. Serve with vinegar soaked chilies, sweet chili sauce and cucumber.

GRILLED THAI MACKEREL

BPLAA TUU YANG

SERVES 4

Bplaa Tuu is the Thai national fish that is highly favored. Although *Bplaa Tuu* (Thai mackerel) is difficult to find outside of Thailand, any locally-caught mackerel will suffice. It is served with a platter of vegetables and relishes and usually shared with a group of people. It is quite time consuming to make but is well worth the effort. Any cooked or fresh vegetables and herbs can be served with this dish.

6 Thai mackerel or yellow fin
    mackerel
pinch of salt
baby cucumbers, hand broken
fresh Thai chilies
1 bunch of snake beans, blanched

1 handful Thai eggplants
3 boiled salted duck eggs (page 26)
oyster omelet (page 28)
1 bunch Vietnamese mint
1 bunch Thai Basil
1 bunch sawtooth coriander

1 iceberg lettuce
roasted tomato relish (page 36)
roast banana pepper relish (page 37)
pork lon (*Lon Naem*, page 46)
sticky rice (page 31)
roti (page 29)

Make all the relishes a day in advance. Keep in the refrigerator until needed.

Light the coals if using a coal grill or use barbecue grill.

Place a small amount of sea salt on the fish and then grill for 10 to 15 minutes. Allow to rest.

While the fish is cooking, place all the other ingredients onto a platter. Heat the two relishes. Heat the roti in a pan with a little oil or butter until golden.

Serve the fish on a plate with the platter of sides.

THAI DESSERTS
AND DRINKS

STICKY RICE WITH MANGO

KAAO NIEW MAMUANG

SERVES 4–5

This dessert would have to be the most famous Thai dessert, sold in almost every Thai restaurant around the world. Its creamy texture with the softness of the sticky rice, the sweet refreshing taste of the mango—it really is heaven on a plate!

    600 ml (1 pint) coconut cream
    250 g (8 oz) castor sugar
    2 teaspoons salt
    1 fresh pandan leaf
    5 mangos, sliced thinly
    900 g (1½ pints) hot, freshly cooked sticky rice

Make the sticky rice as per instructions (page 31).

In a saucepan, add the coconut cream, sugar, salt and pandan leaf. Heat and simmer for 5 minutes. Allow to cool completely.

Add the hot sticky rice to a small bowl. Pour in half of the coconut mix and combine with the rice.

Spoon the sticky rice on to serving plates. Top with the sliced mango. Spoon the rest of the coconut mix over the top and serve.

BANANA IN COCONUT MILK WITH TAPIOCA PEARLS

GLUAY BUAT CHII SAA KUU

SERVES 3–4

Gluay Buat Chii Saa Kuu is an amazing dessert that is creamy and rich, the banana must be *Gluay Nahm Wah* as they are more starchy then the western bananas and hold their shape while cooking.

    1 L (32 fl oz) coconut milk
    125 g (4 oz) castor sugar
    1 teaspoon of salt
    300 ml (10 fl oz) filtered water
    6 Thai bananas, whole
    125 g (4 oz) tapioca pearls (store purchased)
    1 pandas leaf, fresh

Fill a pot with water and bring to the boil. Add the tapioca pearls. Once the tapioca is clear all the way through (there is no sign of a white middle), take off the heat and strain. Keep running water until the tapioca is completely cool. Leave in a bowl with a small amount of water (the water will help the tapioca not to stick).

In a pot, add the water and sugar. Bring to the boil and reduce to a simmer to make a syrup. Once the syrup has reduced by half, add the coconut milk and salt. Add the bananas and pandas leaf. Bring to a light simmer and cook for 4–5 minutes or just until the banana becomes soft. Remove from heat.

Add tapioca pearls to serving bowls and top with the coconut cream. Share the bananas between each serving.

Thai Food Sensation

BANANA AND STICKY RICE WITH CARAMELIZED COCONUT

KAAO TOM MAT

SERVES 3–4

This is an amazing dessert that does take a little work but it is worth the effort. The banana and sticky rice are steamed together in the banana leaf to make a little parcel of joy. All the flavor is kept inside the leaf and becomes somewhat like a rice pudding.

500 g (16 oz) glutinous rice, soaked
    in water overnight
300 ml (10 fl oz) coconut milk
100 ml (3 fl oz) coconut cream
½ teaspoon salt
185 g (6 oz) palm sugar

2 coconuts, flesh only grated
10 tablespoons palm sugar (or cane
    sugar)
180 ml (6 fl oz) coconut milk
½ teaspoon salt
1 teaspoon tapioca flour

4 tablespoons palm sugar
1 pandus leaf
5 Thai bananas, cut in half
    lengthwise and then crossways
6 banana leaves

Soak the sticky rice overnight, strain the rice and place it into a saucepan. Add the coconut milk and cream, the salt and sugar. Bring to a light simmer and cook for 4 to 6 minutes or until the milk and cream have been absorbed and the rice is thick (risotto consistency). Once the rice is ready, remove from saucepan and place onto a tray to cool for around 10 minutes.

Place the banana leaf onto the gas flame to release the oil, then set aside to slightly cool.

Take a banana leaf, place one large tablespoon of rice mixture in the center, and place the banana on the top of the rice. Fold the banana leaf over the top, and then fold in the sides. Bring a Thai sticky rice steamer to a rapid boil. Once the steamer is boiling, place the parcels into the steamer and steam for 30 minutes.

To make the caramelized coconut threads, add the palm sugar to a large saucepan. Heat until it forms a light caramel. Add the grated coconut and cook for 2 minutes. Remove and place onto a tray.

To make the coconut sauce, add the coconut milk, sugar, salt and pandas leaf to a saucepan. Bring to the boil. In a small bowl combined the tapioca flour with 3 tablespoon of coconut milk to make the flour runny. Once the cream comes to a boil, turn the heat down and add the flour. Cook until slightly thicker.

Once the rice parcels are cooked, top with the caramelized coconut threads and the coconut sauce.

Thai Food Sensation

PUMPKIN AND LYCHEE IN COCONUT MILK

FAK TONG GANG BUAD

SERVES 3–4

This dessert works so well with the sweetness of the lychee and the rich balance of the coconut milk.

900 ml (1½ pints) coconut milk
1 teaspoon salt
125 g (4 oz) palm sugar
125 g (4 oz) castor sugar

250 ml (8 fl oz) coconut cream
1 pandas leaf
1 kabocha pumpkin or ½ a small
   Japanese pumpkin

1 tin Thai lychee or 300 g (10 oz)
   fresh lychee

In a medium saucepan combine the coconut milk, salt, pandas leaf and both sugars together. Heat gradually over a low heat then simmer for 5 to 10 minutes. Stir occasionally to mix help the sugars dissolve.

Peel and chop the pumpkin into 1½ cm (½ inch) pieces. Add pumpkin to the coconut milk and bring back to the simmer. Add in the lychee. Stir lightly so that the pumpkin does not mash. Cook until the pumpkin is tender but still holding together. Add the coconut cream and bring to a light simmer once more then remove from heat.

Serve the dessert warm.

BLACK STICKY RICE SWEET CORN AND CARAMEL PEANUTS

KAAO NIEW DAHM

SERVES 4

250 g (8 oz) black glutinous rice,
    soaked in water overnight
1 L (1¾ pints) cold water
3 pandan leaves
1 teaspoon salt
125 g (4 oz) palm sugar
2 corn cobs

The sauce
500 ml (16 fl oz) coconut milk
2 tablespoons rice flour
2 teaspoons salt

Nut crumble
4 tablespoons castor sugar
4 tablespoons palm sugar
125 g (4 oz) roasted peanuts,
    crushed

Drain the rice overnight and cook in steamer on different levels. Add the corn cob to the steamer and steam for 35 minutes. Cool and remove the corn from the cob. Discard the core.

In a saucepan bring the water and palm sugar to a simmer. Add the pandas leaves, coconut milk and salt. Simmer for 5 minutes to create a stock. Add a small amount of water to the rice flour and mix well to form a paste. Add the rice flour paste to the stock and thicken slightly.

Add the castor and palm sugars to a saucepan and heat until it forms a light caramel. Add the crushed peanuts. Turn off the heat and slowly combine the caramel with the nuts. Place onto a tray lined with banking paper and allow to cool. Once cool, place into a mortar and pound to a rough crumble.

Ladle a spoon full of the pudding into each serving bowl. Pour the stock over the top and finish with 2 tablespoons of peanuts and a sprinkle of sweet corn. Serve with ice cream if desired.

TAPIOCA WITH SWEET CORN, BLACK GRASS JELLY AND COCONUT MILK

KHANOM WAN RUAM MIT

SERVES 2–3

Khanom Wan Ruam Mit is a very yummy dessert that kids love. The fun with the tapioca keeps kids happy. The creamy coconut broth is full of flavor with a hint of salt and pandas leaf.

220 g (7 oz) tapioca pearls (store purchased)
500 ml (16 fl oz) coconut milk

300 ml (10 fl oz) sugar syrup (page 31)
1 pandas leaf
pinch of salt

500 g (16 oz) black grass jelly, diced
3 whole corn cobs, steamed
8–10 ice cubes
roasted coconut

Fill a pot with water and bring to the boil. Add the tapioca pearls. Once the tapioca is clear all the way through (there is no sign of a white middle), take off the heat and strain. Keep running water until the tapioca is completely cool. Leave in a bowl with a small amount of water (the water will help the tapioca not to stick).

Bring the salt, pandas leaf and coconut milk to the boil. Turn down the heat and allow to simmer for 10 minutes. Cool to room temperature then add the sugar syrup.

Remove the kernels from the corn and set aside.

Spoon the tapioca into bowls. Add the streamed corn kernels, black jelly and the ice cubes top with the coconut stock.

ROTI STUFFED WITH BANANA

ROTI GLUAY

Roti Gluay is a awesome dessert or snack at any time of the day. The secret is to make the roti yourself. It's not difficult and doesn'tt take too long. Roti needs 12 hours to rest before cooking.

roti (page 29)
The filling
6 gluay nahm wah bananas, sliced
2 egg yolks
4 tablespoons palm sugar
6 tablespoons coconut cream
1 teaspoon salt
2 tablespoons maple syrup (optional)

Place the sliced banana into a bowl. Using a folk, smash up the banana and add the other ingredients. Mix well. Set aside until needed.

Slowly heat the roti pan or frypan. Place the prepared roti in the pan and cook on a medium heat for 5 minutes on each side or until the roti is golden.

While the roti is still in the pan, spoon the filling into the middle then quickly fold in the sides to make a square parcel.

Remove from the pan and cut into bite size pieces.

Serve on a plate or in a bowl and top with condensed milk and sugar (or chocolate hazelnut spread or any other spread of choice such as maple syrup).

Serve immediately.

LEMONGRASS DRINK

MAKES 4

A refreshing drink, this is packed full of fresh lemongrass and mint. It is a very easy and quick drink to make on a hot summer's day.

    5 lemongrass stalks
    1 L (32 fl oz) cold water
    1 drop pandaus extract
    125 ml (4 fl oz) sugar syrup (page 31)
    9 mint leaves
    3 handfuls ice cubes

Add the lemongrass, water and pandaus extract to a bar blender. Blitz on high speed for 3 minutes. Strain the liquid twice through very fine muslin cloth. Add the sugar syrup then pour onto the ice cubes. Serve with a mint leaf.

BANANA SMOOTHIE

MAKES 2

A great drink that is an oldie but a goodie and one that I love to drink on a hot day. Thai banana are very sweet and a lot more flavorful.

    250 g (8 oz) banana
    125 ml (4 fl oz) water
    3 tablespoons sugar syrup (page 31)
    100 ml (3 fl oz) coconut milk
    15 ice cubes
    mint leaves, to garnish

Place all the ingredients into a grinder and blend until smooth. Serve immediately.

THAI ICED TEA

CHA YEN

SERVES 4

Thais love iced tea because the heat in Thailand is so intense. This is a wonderful way to have a sugar hit and a cool down.

  1 L (32 fl oz) of water
  125 g (4 oz) Thai tea
  375 ml (12 fl oz) sugar syrup (page 31)
  250 ml (8 fl oz) condensed milk
  4 handfuls crushed ice

Bring the water to the boil. Add the tea and stir for 2 minutes. Remove from heat and allow to rest for 5 minutes. Fill 4 long glasses with ice. Pour the glass halfway with tea. Add equal amounts of sugar syrup to each glass and 3 tablespoons of condensed milk. Stir and serve.

THAI ICED COFFEE

KAH- FE YEN

SERVES 4

  1L (32 fl oz) water
  60 g (2 oz) Thai coffee powder
  500 ml (16 fl oz) sugar syrup (page 31)
  4 ice cubes (per glass)
  3 tablespoons condensed milk
  fresh milk

In a large saucepan boil the water, then add the coffee powder. Keep on a high flame for 1 minute then set aside to cool completely.

Strain the coffee through a very fine sieve. Add the sugar syrup.

Add ice cubes to each glass. Add 1 tablespoon of condensed milk then add the coffee syrup. Top up with fresh milk and serve.

Measurements

Mass conversions (rounded out)

Metric	Imperial	Cups
10 g	⅓ oz	
15 g	½ oz	
20 g	¾ oz	
30 g	1 oz	
40 g	1½ oz	
60 g	2 oz	¼ cup
75 g	2½ oz	
90 g	3 oz	
100 g	3½ oz	
125 g	4 oz	½ cup 4 tablespoons
150 g	5 oz	
180 g	6 oz	
200 g	7 oz	
220 g	7¾ oz	
250 g	8 oz	1 cup
280 g	9 oz	
300 g	10 oz	
330 g	11 oz	
350 g	11½ oz	
375 g	12 oz	
400 g	14 oz	
425 g	15 oz	
460 g	15½ oz	
500 g	16 oz (1 lb)	
600 g	1 lb 5 oz	
700 g	1 lb 7 oz	
750 g	1 lb 8 oz	
800 g	1 lb 10 oz	
1 kg	2 lb	
1.5 kg	3 lb	
2 kg	4 lb	

Thai Food Sensation

Volume conversions (rounded out)

Metric	Imperial	Cups
30 ml	1 fl oz	
60 ml	2 fl oz	¼ cup
75 ml	2½ fl oz	
90 ml	3 fl oz	⅓ cup
125 ml	4 fl oz	½ cup
150 ml	5 fl oz	⅔ cup
180 ml	6 fl oz	¾ cup
200 ml	6¾ fl oz	
220 ml	7 fl oz	
250 ml	8 fl oz	1 cup
300 ml	10 fl oz	
375 ml	12 fl oz	
400 ml	13 fl oz	
440 ml	14 fl oz	
500 ml	16 fl oz (1 pint)	
625 ml	1¼ pints	
750 ml	24 fl oz (1½ pints)	
875 ml	1¾ pints	
1 L	32 fl oz (2 pints)	

TEMPERATURES

Celsius	Fahrenheit
100°C	225°F
125°C	250°F
150°C	300°F
160°C	325°F
170°C	325°F
180°C	350°F
190°C	375°F
200°C	400°F
210°C	425°F
220°C	425°F
230°C	450°F
250°C	500°F

ABBREVIATIONS

g	gram
kg	kilogram
mm	millimetre
cm	centimetre
ml	millilitre
°C	degrees Celsius

CAKE TIN SIZES

Metric	Imperial/US
15 cm	6 inches
18 cm	7 inches
20 cm	8 inches
23 cm	9 inches
25 cm	10 inches
28 cm	11 inches

Glossary of Thai Ingredients

Apple Eggplants—Makreua Prao

Apple eggplants come in a range of colors; green, yellow, purple and orange. Small in size and round, they look more like small radishes. Buying apple eggplants as fresh as possible will give you the best outcome, as the eggplants still need to be firm once cooked.

Bamboo Shoots—Nor Mai

Bamboo shoots must be picked at a young age. The best time to eat young bamboo shoots is when freshly harvested. Bamboo does "turn" very quickly due to the acid and sugars reacting to one another that turn the bamboo shoot into an extremely bitter and rancid product.

Bananas—Gluay

There are 28 varieties of bananas in Thailand each with their own different taste and texture. The cooking methods range from grilling to deep frying. Different bananas have more starch content than others, allowing the banana to be grilled for a longer period of time without the banana turning soft and gluggy.

Banana Blossom—Hua Blii

Banana blossoms are the purple buds of the plant that contain the sterile flowers. The taste is sappy yet bitter and mostly used in curries and salads. To prepare the bud for cooking, the outer layer must be removing, take out the white heart and remove the stamens by shaking the blossom. Add to salted or citrus water to keep from deoxidizing.

Banana Leaf—Bai Dtong

The leaves of the banana tree are mostly used to wrap food but occasionally to hold together desserts and rice.

Holy Basil—Bai Grapao

The Thai people have two types of holy basil, white and red. The red variety has purple stalks and is more pungent. The white variety has green stalks and is less pungent; mostly used in seafood curries and soups. The red holy basil is mostly used in curries and stir-fries.

Lemon Basil—Bai Manglaek

This basil is small and has light green leaves that smell just like lemon; mostly used in wet dishes and curries.

Thai Basil—Bai Horapha

This is a purple-stemmed green leaf herb with a heavy aniseed fragrance and a strong taste of liquorice. Thai basil adds freshness and sweetness to curries and stir-fries; mostly used in red curries and green curries, stir-fries and soups.

Bentel Leaves—Bai Champluu

Bentel leaves, also known as pepper leaves, are a small green leaf used as a base for snacks and meat products.

Bean Sprouts—Thua Ngok

There are a few types of bean sprouts, from soybean spouts to mung bean sprouts. Mung bean sprouts can be found in the refrigeration section of the supermarket.

Cardamom—Luk Grawan

Cardamom is a spice that is used in very small quantities, mostly used in curries. When preparing the cardamom, use a dry pan to heat the cardamom pod to release the aroma.

Cassia Bark—Op Choey

Cassia bark is related to the cinnamon family. The quills are larger and more coarse with a much richer flavor. It can be found in any good Asian grocery store.

Celery—Keun Chai

Asian celery is a lot stronger than the western celery. It looks a lot like flat leaf parsley. Great in stir-fries and soups.

Chilies—Phrik

Chilies come is all shapes and sizes. The rule of thumb; the smaller the chilies, the more hotter it will be. Before using a chili, a good idea would be to have a small bite so you can determine the heat.

Coconut—Mapraow

The coconut tree can be found everywhere in Thailand and fresh coconut is the best. When buying the coconut, buy the heaviest for its size, as it means more water and fresher. Coconuts can be eaten fresh or cooked on open coals.

Cilantro—Pak Chii

Cilantro is an herb that is fresh and vibrant. When cooking with cilantro, the whole herb is used, roots and all. The roots are mostly used in soups, curries and pastes. The leaves are used to give aroma.

Cilantro Seed—Luuk Pak Chii

Cilantro seeds come from the cilantro plant. Thai cilantro seeds have more flavor and are smaller then the other cilantro seeds on the market. Before using, dry fry in a pan so that the seeds release their oils and aroma.

Durian—Turian

This is the most "notorious" fruit in Thailand; it is loved or hated. The fruit has a very strong and pungent smell that some describe as baby vomit while others describe it as sweet and extremely yummy.

Eggplant—Makreua

Thailand has a few different types of eggplants. The best way to prepare the eggplants is to cut the eggplant and then place in salted water—not too long as the eggplant will become waterlogged. Salting the eggplant will help the eggplant not to turn brown.

Fish Sauce—Nahm BPlaa

Fish sauce is the Thai version of salt that is the foundation of seasoning any dish. The fish sauce could be made from cuttlefish, sardines, fish or shrimp (prawns) that have been salted and left for two years in large underground barrels to marinate. The quality of fish sauce differs with the brand. It is extremely pungent while others are more mild.

Galangl—Khaa

Galangal is a part of the ginger family called rhizomes. The younger the galangal the less pungent. Use young galangal in soups. The older and darker colored galangal is used in curry pastes for its strong peppery flavor.

Ground Roasted Rice—Kao Krua

Used as a texture binder for salads and dipping sauces, this rice best known from the salad called *Larb*. The process to making roasted rice is to heat a dry pan and on high heat, add the uncooked white sticky rice and cook until golden. Pound to a fine powder.

Jackfruit—Kanun

Jackfruit is the largest single fruit on the planet; very similar appearance to the durian. Sweet in taste, it is used in savory and sweet dishes.

Kaffir Lime—Bai Makrut

The fruit and leaves of this citrus tree are used extensively throughout Thailand, from seasoning soups to curries. This little fruit is full of flavor, which is extremely strong and slightly bitter. Fresh is always best for this ingredient.

Lemongrass—Dtakrai

Lemongrass is an amazing plant that is extremely versatile and used in many Thai dishes. This blade-like plant is used in curries and soups.

Limes—Manao

Thai limes are smaller and sweeter then the western counterparts. Use fresh.

Mango—Mamuang

Mango trees can be found everywhere in Thailand. Used mostly for sweets such as mango sticky rice, they can be added to salads and curries.

Mint—Bai Sarae Nae

Thais use mint just like any other country to flavor their salads and dressings.

Pandanus Leaf—Bai Dtoei Horm

Pandanus is a leaf that is dark green and normally sold in bunches. The fresh leaves are used to flavor desserts. It is known as the Asian vanilla bean.

Pea Eggplant—Makreua Puang

Pea eggplants look like little green peas. Their taste is a little bitter and has a wonderful "pop" feeling when eaten. They are quite strong on the palate but together with all the other ingredients, they blend nicely; mostly added to green curries.

Red Shallots—Horn Dtaeng

Thai shallots are smaller than western shallots and somewhat sweeter. They are used mostly in curries, salads and dressings. They can be fresh, dried or deep-fried.

Shrimp Paste—Gapi

Shrimp paste is the most important ingredient in Thailand. It is made of shrimp that has been salted and fermented. It is known to be the soul of Thai ingredients giving body to the dish.

Snake Beans—Tua Fak Yao

Known by two names, snake bean or yard-long bean, it is used in stir-fires, salads and curries. They are a great ingredient to garnish relishes. Can be found served on a side plate ready to be eaten raw.

Tamarind—Makaam Sot

Tamarind is the pulp contained in a brown outer bean-like pod. It can be sweet or sour and is used for seasoning curries to soups and dressings. Tamarind is used as the sour element of Thai cuisine.

Tapioca—Saku

Tapioca is used to thicken soups and desserts. These little pearls are white but once cooked became a clear ball.

Wild Ginger—Grachai

Grachai is also a part of the ginger family known as Rhizome. Grachai is known mostly as a wild ginger that is added to curry pastes and soups, mostly with a seafood base dish.

Index

Acknowledgements

There are many people I would like to thank for all their support, not just in helping with *Thai Food Sensation*, but also my life.

Firstly to my wife Sirawan, thank you for your support, love and friendship. I believe I am a better man and a better husband and father due to being with you. You have given me so much and I thank you and love you very much. To my little babies, Elliya and Andre, you are my world. I love being with you and watching you grow. One day we will all be cooking together.

To Sirawan's family in Thailand and Australia, thank you for teaching me all the secrets of Thai cooking and culture, for your love and kindness and for opening your arms to me and teaching me about the country of Thailand. My heart knows where home is.

To my family in Australia for their love and support, thank you.

Thank you to Evelyn Lundstrom for all your help in advising me and for your help in setting up the *Thai Food Sensation* Facebook page. Your professional approach has helped me in so many different areas. Your time that you gave to me will always be remembered.

Thank you to my first head chef, Alain Carbonie. You still are a crazy Frenchman but I will never forget the training and advice you gave me when I was 13 years old. Thanks to Taz for giving me my first ever job in hospitality at a very young age; thank you to David, Alan and everyone else at the bakery.

To all the boys whom I worked with at Bathers' Pavilion, for there friendship and support; it's so awesome knowing you all and having worked beside you all.

A very huge thank you to Andrew Norman and Jason Leggatt. Andy, you're a true blue Englishman whom I love being around. Your friendship is a blessing and one that has been a lot of fun.

Jason your guidance, passion for life and energy is huge; the old days were the best and I will never forget the times we shared.

To New Holland Publishing for the opportunity to publish my own book; the team at New Holland are the very best in the industry and for that I'm very grateful.

To Chris and Nick from Poseidon Oyster & Seafood for all the freshest seafood for *Thai Food Sensation*. Your produce is what makes me love being a chef.

Thank you to all that have helped me in the past, present and future, thank you.

First published in 2015 by New Holland Publishers Pty Ltd
London • Sydney • Auckland

The Chandlery Unit 704 50 Westminster Bridge Road London SE1 7QY United Kingdom
1/66 Gibbes Street Chatswood NSW 2067 Australia
5/39 Woodside Ave Northcote, Auckland 0627 New Zealand

www.newhollandpublishers.com

A record of this book is held at the British Library and the National Library of Australia.

ISBN 9781742576305

Managing Director: Fiona Schultz
Publisher: Linda Williams
Project Editor: Susie Stevens
Designer: Peter Guo
Proofreader: Jessica McNamara
Production Director: Olga Dementiev
Photographer: Greg Ellis
Printer: Toppan Leefung Printing Limited

10 9 8 7 6 5 4 3 2 1

Keep up with New Holland Publishers on Facebook
www.facebook.com/NewHollandPublishers